# THE DAY THE MUSIC DIED

## A Rock'n'Roll Tribute

D1493018

Plexus, London

Published by Plexus Publishing Limited
26 Dafforne Road
London SW17 8TZ
First printing 1989

The Day the music died : a rock and roll tribute

1. Rock music   History and criticism
784.5′4   ML 3534

ISBN 0-85965-059-6
ISBN 0-85965-058-8 Pbk

Typeset by St George Typesetting, Redruth, Cornwall
Printed in Great Britain by Hollen Street Press

# CONTENTS

# ACKNOWLEDGEMENTS

*The Day The Music Died* is the result of a collaborative effort that has spanned several years. It is a tribute and homage to 26 of the most remarkable rock and roll artists of our time who died young and at the same time inspired most of our lives. The book includes contributions by some of the most eminent writers from both sides of the Atlantic who have either personally known the artist they have written about or simply truly appreciated and loved his or her work. Subjectivity, in this case, does not make for a warped view of history, but rather a more personal one.

We would like, therefore, to give special thanks to all the contributors whose essays make up this book: Chris Charlesworth, John Collis, Cameron Crowe, David Dalton, Brian Edge, Mick Farren, Ben Fong-Torres, David Fricke, Simon Frith, Paulo Hewitt, Jerry Hopkins, Patrick Humphries, Nick Kent, Greil Marcus, Gavin Martin, Philip Norman, Mark Paytress, Bud Scoppa, Charles Shaar Murray, John Swenson, John Tobler, Cliff White and Timothy White.

The following essays appear by kind permission of:
Greil Marcus ''Keith Moon. The Different Drummer'' from *Rolling Stone* magazine 19 October 1978. Reprinted by permission of Straight Arrow Publishers, Inc © 1978.
Philip Norman: ''John Lennon'' from *Shout. The True Story Of The Beatles.* Copyright © 1980 by Philip Norman. Reprinted by permission of the Peters, Fraser and Dunlop Group Ltd.
Timothy White ''Bob Marley'' © Copyright 1981, 1982 by Timothy White. All rights reserved by the author. Originally appeared in slightly different version in *Rolling Stone* magazine.

We would like to thank the following individuals for their collaboration editorially: Nicky Adamson, Paul Rambali, Debbie Geller, Charlie Gillet, Chris Charlesworth, Pete Basset, Roberta Cruger of MCA and Ken Kitchen for his cover design.

We would also like to thank the following individuals and picture agencies who contributed to the gathering of photographs for this book: Apple Records, Granada Television, Elektra Records, WEA Records, A&M Records, Phonogram, CBS Records, Motown Records, RCA, MCA, EMI, Liberty Records, Capricorn Records, Chuck Pulin, Dezo Hoffman, Barry Plummer, Ian Dickson, Chris Walter/Relay Photos, Fin Costello, Denise Richardson, Neal Preston, Terry O'Neill/Camera Press, Neil Jones, Gary Herman, United Artists, Harry Hammond, Ariola International, ABKCO, Rob Burt, Kevin Cummins, Island Records, Syndication International, Andre Csillag/Relay Photos, Jim Marshall, Camera Press, Topix, Gered Mankowitz, Terence Donovan/Camera Press, David Bonner, Debbie Kirby of Echoes, David Bailey/Camera Press, Decca, Associated Newspapers, National Film Archive, Jan Persson, Ron Reid/Camera Press, Tom Hanley/Camera Press, Robert Freeman/Camera Press, Ben Ross/Camera Press, Blue Mountain, Warner Bros, Denis O'Regan, Trinifold, The Music Library, Popperfoto, Stax Records, MCA Records, Walt Davidson, Bob Gruen, Glitterbest, Bob Leafe, Record Mirror, Sounds Archive and Sharon Davies.

It has not been possible in all cases to trace the copyright sources, and the publishers would be glad to hear from any such unacknowledged copyright holders.

# Duane Allman

## 20 November 1946 - 29 October 1971

## by Cameron Crowe

*Duane Allman was born in Nashville, Tennessee on 20 November 1946. After gaining a local reputation as the Allman Joys, Duane and his brother, Gregg, joined a studio band – Hourglass – in Los Angeles in the late sixties. Duane's success on Wilson Pickett's 'Hey Jude' led to a firm fixture as a session man with Muscle Shoal's Fame Studio (backing Aretha Franklin among others), and the birth of the Allman Brothers Band. Their debut album was released to critical acclaim in New York and Duane's personal reputation increased. Universally recognized as one of the world's leading exponents of bottleneck guitar, his career was cut short by a fatal motorcycle accident in Macon, Georgia on 29 October 1971.*

Duane Allman had been dead almost two years when I first met the Allman Brothers Band in 1973. I was sixteen, and it was my first major assignment for *Rolling Stone* magazine. The Allman Brothers were my favourite band, and I was not to be stopped. After ten days on the road with the group, I'd seen every show and taped long interviews with everyone from the lighting crew to singer-organist Gregg Allman.

The band's publicist had said in advance that the tragic motorcycle

death of Duane Allman was a subject not to be discussed, but every interview and every conversation had eventually turned back to that sad topic. They were pained and heartfelt interviews, and I was amazed that the band and crew had been so open with me. The night before I was to leave the tour and write the story, I knew I had something special.

At four that morning, my hotel room phone rang. I was sharing the room with photographer Neal Preston, and Neal picked up the

phone. He mumbled a few sentences in a low, nervous voice. I instantly knew something was wrong.

Neal hung up and switched on the desk lamp. 'Gregg wants you to come to his room,' he said. 'He wants you to bring him all your interview tapes, right now.'

A cold fear crept through me. Gregg Allman had been friendly to me, but many others had warned that he was distant and moody. I wondered about the possible psychology of such a close-knit group as the Allman Brothers: an outsider had killed Duane, now another outsider wanted to write about it. I gathered all but one of the fifteen interview tapes and headed upstairs to Allman's room. I still remember shaking so hard that I dropped the tapes in the elevator.

Allman answered the door himself. He was solemn, his long blond hair was pressed against his head with perspiration. His eyes were fixed on some distant point as he led me inside.

'Let me see your i.d.', he said. 'You could be anybody – hanging

*Duane Allman, pioneer of southern rock, at New York's Central Park Music Festival in 1971.*

around, asking us questions. We told you everything. It's all on those cassettes.' He looked over to an empty chair across the room. I clenched my teeth together to keep them from chattering. 'Duane's in the room right now. He's sitting there and he's laughing at you.'

I noticed an empty whisky bottle on the table and so I didn't want to argue with Allman. It was a strange and astonishing transformation he had gone through. I gave him all the tapes, and went home the next day believing I'd lost the story. Too many personal questions, too much naïveté on my part.

But Gregg Allman woke up the next day and called his roadie. 'Why do I have these tapes,' he wanted to know. The tapes were sent back to me the next day, along with a soul-searching eight-page biographical letter written by Allman. I wrote the story, and never alluded to the incident Gregg Allman would call 'a nightmare I can't exactly remember'. He would go through his mother's scrapbooks to help send early photos for my article, and I would write about the Allmans many times after that, but we would never discuss that incident over the tapes.

I understood, even then. Gregg Allman was still Duane's younger brother. And Duane Allman, besides being one of the first modern rockers to rise out of the South, was a powerful young man. A charismatic 'father of the family' to the Allman Brothers Band, he died at the very peak of his career. He'd been recording from 1966 to the summer of 1971 and Duane had just seen his first gold record arrive for the seminal *Live At Fillmore East* album. After his death, the band was left without its inspiration and without its leader. That the Allman Brothers Band were able to continue after Duane, and rise to even greater success without him, is one of the modern miracles of rock.

It's conceivable that Duane Allman will always be remembered as a self-contained stereotype – the pioneer of southern rock. But like John Lydon and punk rock after him, Allman encapsulated a *personality* as well as a genre. Duane Allman had an Attitude. Forget the South – Allman knew he was one of the hottest guitar players to come down the pike, period. Besides forming the Allman Brothers Band and guiding them to nationwide success on his own terms, Allman's confidence also helped loosen the tightest of musical fraternities, the session men.

In the year or so before the first Allmans album, Duane was a studio guitar demon. Under the guidance of producer Jerry Wexler, and Muscle Shoals Fame Studio's master Rick Hall, Duane powered the sessions behind some of the most influential soul, blues and rock of the sixties and early seventies. Listen to Aretha Franklin's 'The Weight', or Boz Scaggs' 'Somebody Loan Me A Dime', and then listen to Clapton's 'Layla'. It could well be the work of three different guitarists, but the spark is unmistakably Duane. Those who knew and worked with him can tell a thousand stories about the long-haired blond kid who stepped in with the catfish-eating professionals and kicked ass. From the very beginning, it appeared that Duane Allman's success was pre-ordained. But sadly, tragedy also seemed to form an integral part of his short life.

Duane Allman was born in Nashville, Tennessee, on 20 November 1946. His younger brother, Gregg, was born the next year. In 1949, the boys' father, a first lieutenant in the army, returned home from the Korean War for the holidays. The day after Christmas, Mr Allman picked up a hitchhiker who turned out to be a dangerous mental case and murdered him.

'You've got to consider why anybody wants to become a musician anyway,' Gregg had said in our first interview. 'I always played for peace of mind.'

Left as the breadwinner, Geraldine Allman sent the boys to Castle Heights Military Academy in Lebanon, Tennessee, while she studied to be an accountant. In 1958, the family moved to Daytona Beach, Florida. Duane was rapidly becoming a problem child but by contrast in the summer of 1960, thirteen-year-old Gregg took a nice summer job as a paperboy. He went to Sear's department store one day for a pair of gloves, but his attention was diverted by a display of guitars. He bought a guitar instead.

That same summer, Duane had purchased a motorcycle, a small Harley 165, and earned himself the title of 'Terror of the Neighbourhood'. 'He was a real bastard as a kid,' said Gregg. 'He quit school I don't know how many times. But he always had that motorcycle, and drove it till it fell apart. When it did, he quit school for good.'

Duane then traded the motorcycle parts in for a guitar like his brother's. Gregg gave his older brother his first few lessons, and Duane took to the guitar with typical zeal. Instead of returning to school, Duane stayed at home and listened to the local R&B station, studying Chuck Berry and Robert Johnson records. And then Duane finally began to read. Voraciously. In later years, he would do his brother's Physics homework so Gregg could make band gigs.

After a year of practice, Duane and Gregg were ready to perform. Their first bands were variously known as the Shufflers, the Escorts, the Y-Teens and the Houserockers. They became regional legends on looks alone. There, in the toughest black bars of Florida, was a blues-rock duo with two angelic-looking faces playing songs like 'I

Feel Good'.

Tom Petty, then an under-age upstart living in Jacksonville, remembers hoisting himself up on a cement wall to see a frat dance where Duane and Gregg, then called the Allman Joys, appeared in 1966. 'Duane just stood there, off to the side, ripping through these great leads,' recalls Petty, 'and there was his little baby-faced brother who opened his mouth and sounded like Joe Tex.'

It was on a long tour of what Duane called 'the garbage circuit of the South' that the band ran into the high-riding Nitty Gritty Dirt Band in the airport. The Dirt Band's manager, Bill McCuen, told the Allmans to give up the roadwork, to come to California and really get serious.

Gregg was suspicious – those regional crowds were awful comfortable – but Duane was ready for the shot. Gregg relented, and off to California they went. It all seemed too good to be true, and in fact it was. The record label, Liberty, re-named the group Hourglass, ordered the band to dress in imitation Paul Revere clothing, and told them not to play live in order to preserve the band's mystique. Amazingly, they complied for over a year. Their material was chosen for them on the only two Hourglass albums. 'Together,' said Gregg, 'those two records form what is known as a shit sandwich.'

It was the ultimate embarrassment for a proud kid like Duane Allman. In one of the band's few clandestine live dates, they had acquired the favourable attention of Neil Young, then of the Buffalo Springfield, who wrote liner notes on the second Hourglass album. For a while, Young's respect was all that kept them going. The band were soon forced to hop to several low-rent motels to escape mounting bills and it was at one such flop house in Hollywood that Gregg had wandered past an open door. Lying

*Duane and Gregg (second and third left) with the Allman Brothers Band.*

there was a dead man, a suicide case, with a sheet pulled over him. He'd taken 95 Seconals and left a note. It was an ugly reminder of what had become of their careers as Hourglass. And that is where Duane drew the line.

'Duane got fed up and when my brother got fed up, he got *fed up*,' said Gregg. ' ''Fuck this,'' he kept yelling. ''Fuck this whole thing. Fuck wearing these weird clothes. Fuck playing this 'In A Gadda Da Vida' shit. Fuck it all!'' '

The band packed up and headed for Muscle Shoals, Alabama, where Duane paid to have some of their own material taped without outside interference. It was fiery blues, like the old days, and some of the tracks would appear years later on the two fine *Duane Allman: An Anthology* albums. (Well worth the search, if you ask around.) After those sessions, Hourglass broke up and the Allmans returned to Jacksonville to re-group.

It would not be that easy. Liberty Records called and threatened to sue for an alleged $48,000 investment in Hourglass. They wanted Gregg. For the first time in their lives, much less careers, Duane and Gregg split. Lawyers forced Gregg to return to L.A. to fulfil the contract while Duane stayed behind. For several weeks, Gregg would be given the rare privilege of watching a 26-piece orchestra cut his first album from songs he had written or chosen himself.

Back at the studios in Muscle Shoals, owner-operator Rick Hall was gearing up for an important Wilson Pickett session, a test audition for Pickett's future recording account. Hall wanted the business, and remembered the hot young guitarist he'd seen recording with Hourglass, so he sent a telegram to Duane Allman in Jacksonville. Duane jumped at the chance of a paid job.

Muscle Shoals, Alabama, was legendary as a straight town. Very tight, very conservative, and very southern, it was also dry: the nearest legal alcohol was over 70 miles away. The good ol' boys were not quite prepared for long-haired Duane Allman to stroll into town wearing his best British bluesman shirts and red, white and blue sneakers.

But is was inevitable that Duane would hit it off with Wilson Pickett. Allman knew Pickett's music backwards and forwards, and Pickett had never been backed by a guitar player like Duane. It was Pickett who gave Duane his studio nickname 'Skydog' – 'Because he hits the heights, man'.

It was Duane who suggested that Pickett recorded 'Hey Jude'. Pickett listened attentively to Duane's idea, but at first responded, 'Hey man, I can't sing that song. I've got a lot of Jewish people working for me!' Eventually enlightened, Pickett cut the track with Duane on lead guitar. It sold a million copies, and Duane was of course invited to stay on in Muscle Shoals as a regular session man. He was the youngest player working there, and culture shock would soon set in.

'It was bullshit,' Duane would remember. 'One of those cats got a 442 Oldsmobile, and then they all had to have one. Then one trades it in on a Tornado and then they all have to have one…I was getting to like it.'

For all the fame he generated in Muscle Shoals, Duane stayed there only six-and-a-half months. In that time, he also mastered the slide guitar. It would become one of his great trademarks. 'Most slide players are muddy,' said Jerry Wexler. 'Their playing sounds sour. Duane is one of the very, very few who played clean, sweet and to the note.'

Allman was suddenly much in demand and soon his showmanship during recording sessions became as legendary as his musical talent. He'd hew and haw, pace and shout,

work himself up into a pitch of energy, and then pick up the guitar. He would scream through two or three takes at the most. Then he'd want to move on. 'It's gone,' he'd say. 'I'll try it again tomorrow.'

As Duane moved out of session work, Rick Hall, who had signed him to an exclusive contract, tried recording a power-trio solo album. The results were mixed, and Duane returned to Jacksonville once again in search of the perfect band. By then, Hall had sold Duane's contract to a young manager named Phil Walden. With Walden's backing, Duane began sleeping on floors and looking for players.

A couple of weeks later, Duane found himself in the middle of a particularly hot jam between himself, local guitarist Dickey Betts, bassist Berry Oakley, and drummers Butch Trucks and Jaimo Johnson. They were playing in a small room at Betts' Commune. The jam went on for three or four hours, and when the music trailed off, Duane looked around the room. 'Man,' he said, 'anybody who ain't in this band has got to fight their way out.'

There was little disagreement among the musicians. All they needed was a singer, and Duane Allman had planned for that. He placed a phone call to California, where a despondent Gregg Allman was considering suicide.

'I had been building the nerve to put a pistol to my head,' Gregg had written in the biographical letter that accompanied my tapes. 'Then Duane called and told me he had a band. He said, "I want you to come down here, round it up and send it somewhere." I put my thumb out and caught the first thing smokin' for Jacksonville.'

Luck was starting to turn in favour of the Allman Brothers Band, as they called themselves. Phil Walden suggested moving the band to Macon, Georgia, where he was setting up Capricorn Records.

They were glad to be out of the competitive Jacksonville scene and enjoyed living in a quieter place where they could improve in private. The band moved a few blocks away from the local college, and lived in a fraternity house while writing the first album. His L.A. experience behind him, Gregg began to blossom as a writer. In short order, Duane had prodded him into finishing a string of future standards like 'Whipping Post', 'Not My Cross To Bear' and 'Midnight Rider'. Much of the other material came from late night sessions with an acoustic guitar, sitting around in nearby Rose Hill Cemetery.

They completed their first album, and the Allman Brothers set out on a rigorous two-year tour, doing nearly 500 dates in one Econoline van. Duane called them the 'Reds, Ripple and Rassaan Roland Kirk days'. They were back on the garbage circuit, but they had a purpose, and more importantly, they had a good time.

The music of the Allman Brothers Band now featured double lead guitars that intertwined hypnotically – almost sexually – in songs that could last for up to 45 minutes. Even then, the music of the Allman Brothers was like backroom bootleg. The feeling between the group and its audience was a strong, and almost forbidden one.

The first few Allman Brothers tours went unnoticed on a national scale. Most of the big-name agents and promoters had seen the group at a Boston showcase, and pronounced them 'too bluesy'. The prevailing opinion as expressed to the band at the time was 'Why are they hiding that blond singer – he should be out front like Tom Jones.' Duane advised the band to forget about it, and keep playing. 'Opinions are like assholes,' he was fond of saying, 'everybody's got one.'

By the time of their second album, *Idlewild South*, a ground swell of concert-going support was gaining for the band. Duane had been paid the ultimate compliment when Eric Clapton invited him to play lead and slide guitar for the *Layla* album. The two became fast friends, and Duane even played a few dates with Derek and the Dominoes, but he never strayed far from the Allman Brothers Band. As the spirit and leader, he also had a new plan for breaking the band wide open. The third album would be the purest of Allman Brothers albums – recorded live at the Fillmore East, Bill Graham's legendary New York rock venue.

*Live at Fillmore East* was released as a double album in 1971, and within two weeks it was tearing up the American charts. The group encountered huge crowds at every stop, and more and more young Southern guitarists would seek out Duane backstage and tell him how he had inspired them to break up their lounge acts and play some *real* music. Duane would smile, sometimes he gave them a guitar. On this incredible high, after two solid years on the road, it seemed time to take a short vacation and enjoy some of the success.

It was during that vacation that Duane Allman was killed. On 29 October 1971 Duane had ridden his motorcycle over to bassist Berry Oakley's house in Macon to wish Oakley's wife Linda a happy birthday. Shortly after leaving the house, at about 5.45pm, he swerved to avoid a truck travelling in the same direction. Duane's cycle skidded and flipped over, dragging him nearly 50 feet. He died of massive injuries after three hours of emergency surgery, at the age of 24.

Duane's death came as a shocking blow to a public which had just taken the Allman Brothers Band to its heart as the premier American band. After Duane's funeral, a moving event attended by most of the artists he had played and

worked with, the Allman Brothers played their first set without him. The original plan was to take six months off, finish the fourth album, and consider the future. But after only four weeks the band reformed and returned to the road. United in grief, they performed some of their best shows ever even if the band's famed two-pronged guitar attack was now only one.

'I used to have nightmares all the time,' said Dickey Betts recently. 'Usually it was the same one. In it, the Allman Brothers Band is on the road, and we end up on a show with Delaney and Bonnie, Duane's old touring buddies. We see Duane at the show, and everything's all right. Duane says, ''Hey man, how've you been?'' And we say ''Great''. And then we all get together and play, and everything's alright again.

'That dream probably kept me sane. Until I could realize what happened. That was about three years later.'

The next album, *Eat A Peach* (a Duane-ism for any interviewer's question about what the band was doing to end the Vietnam War), was a huge success. But death, like popularity, would continue to find the band. Bassist Oakley was just shaking off a year-long depression over Duane, when he too was killed in a motorcycle collision just a few blocks away from the scene of that previous death. He was buried near Duane at Macon's Rose Hill Cemetery.

As the band's concert and album sales continued to mount, the leadership role fell to Duane's younger brother, Gregg. The somewhat shy and quieter brother improved his singing, deepened his songwriting, and added a keyboard player to work on the next album, *Brothers And Sisters*. Typically, the group drowned their sorrow with more hard work. 'Ramblin' Man' became their biggest single ever and the

group made the cover of *Newsweek*. In a music industry eager to follow trends, the door swung wide open for southern rock.

Few of the Allman Brothers Band members have had an easy time in recent years. After leading the band through their most difficult albums, Gregg Allman briefly married Cher and had the unfortunate experience of living in a spotlight of gossip. He bought cars at will, admitted to kicking cocaine and heroin habits, and raised hundreds of thousands of dollars in fund-raising events for Jimmy Carter.

The band broke up for a time during the late seventies, when Gregg felt the need to disappear. He visited his old stomping grounds from the days of the Allman Joys, dated girls he hadn't seen since high school, and tried to live a quiet life. It lasted less than a year. A call came in from Dickey Betts, and Gregg Allman was ready to return.

The Allman Brothers Band reunited in 1979 with several new members, and powerful albums continue. The group still tours regularly, and in every show, according to Butch Trucks, 'we have a place in our set that's for Duane. We all know where it is, and I'm sure he does too.'

I was driving around recently, when I heard a radio interview with Gregg Allman. He seemed sharp and funny, but he also sounded like he'd lived a couple of lifetimes in his nearly 40 years. The interviewer asked him how he reflected on the difficulty of losing his brother, the great Duane Allman. 'As a kid,' Gregg said in reply, 'I always thought an entertainer or a musician would have *no bad days*. How could they? They're entertainers. They have fun for a living. Well, baby, I'm here to tell you they *do* have bad days.' Allman laughed. 'But it ain't nothing I won't feel better about when I'm up on stage tonight.'

# Marc Bolan

## 30 September 1947 - 16 September 1977

## by Mark Paytress

*Marc Bolan was born Mark Feld in Hackney, London, on 30 September 1947. In 1964, he donned a Dylan cap and worked the London folk clubs as Toby Tyler. After a couple of failed singles for Decca as Marc Bolan, he was dropped and met Simon Napier-Bell, then manager of the Yardbirds. Another flop led to a three-month spell rebuilding his ego as guitarist with John's Children in Spring 1967. His confidence restored, Bolan formed Tyrannosaurus Rex with Steve Peregrine Took and built up a solid reputation in 'underground' circles. Took was replaced by Mickey Finn, the duo developed an electric sound and charted with 'Ride A White Swan' in 1970. Having abbreviated their name and expanded to a four-piece, T. Rex chalked up a string of hits during the next three years. By the end of 1973, the group's popularity slumped, and Bolan spent the rest of his career trying to recreate his earlier magic with only limited success. Courted by the new punk movement, he seemed poised to return when he was killed in a car crash in the early hours of 16 September 1977.*

Marc Bolan was rock's first Superstar. Elvis, the Beatles, the Rolling Stones, and countless others before him could claim higher sales or

larger audiences, but when Bolan arrived towards the end of 1970, a new era in rock had begun. The Beatles were no more; and the blues and progressive boom, with its muso posturing and righteous triumph of diligence over style, failed to capture the public imagination. Marc swaggered on centre stage, armed with three chords, a presence which wedded early Presley petulance with lurex Liberace splendour, and restored rock to its former Glam-orous self.

Unhindered by the contradictions

inherent in stardom which bothered his predecessors, Bolan was fêted in the manner of a latter-day Swanson or Valentino. The likes of Hendrix and Joplin, stars as they were, trod carefully so as not to alienate their counter-culture audiences. Jagger did too, though after Altamont his flight from the spotlight was as much a dash for his own physical safety. As for Lennon, he was busy licking his wounds after years of manipulation, and re-emerged with some shrewd but savage conclusions regarding what he felt was the seductive fallacy of fame.

Not so Bolan. Since his earliest days on the streets of Hackney, East London, he had demanded – and received – the attention of those around him. His career had a long gestation period, during which time he adopted several roles: from 'Mod About Town' to quasi-Donovan folkie, garage flower-punk guitarist to pastoral poet of the psychedelic kind. Marc's transition to multi-million-selling 'Bopping Elf' was never inevitable; but throughout his life, he had constantly striven to elevate himself above the Dead

*Marc's soft, angelic features always ensured a good rapport with the camera.*

Joes around him.

The newly-invoked rank of Superstar (created in the wake of the Supergroups' failure at the tail-end of the sixties), was the logical resting place for his self-aggrandizement, and was the role which he played to perfection. The tragedy was that Marc could take it no further, and his subsequent downfall did have more than a glimmer of inevitability about it. His massive overnight success was eventually grounded by a creative lull, and with it, a descent into a diet of food and drugs approaching Presley-like proportions. He had it in the palm of his hand, and he blew it. But while it lasted, T. Rexstasy gave a new generation the opportunity to fulfil its atavistic yearning not only for the swagger and swank of inaugural rock'n'roll, but also the glitz and glamour of the old matinee idols in all their satin and sequinned technicolour glory.

When T. Rex hit big, primal pop was reborn. Yet the remarkable musical formula Bolan established in the months after he went electric was by no means original. 'Get It On', perhaps his biggest worldwide hit, owed much to Chuck Berry's 'Little Queenie', so much so that Marc felt obliged to acknowledge the debt on the fade-out: 'Meanwhile, I'm still thinkin' ', he sang, in his best Berry put-on. In recycling 12-bar rock'n'roll and moulding it into something the press soon dubbed 'glam rock', Bolan marks the meeting place between the Sun Studios, and many of today's chart acts who strive to create a brand of pop as exuberant and as timeless as his own.

Back in 1977, Marc claimed to be 'the original punk' (as did so many old wavers), but this somewhat spurious remark made more

*In 1967 Bolan formed Tyrannosaurus Rex. His lurex splendour created a whole new look in seventies style.*

*The two Gurus of Glam rock: Bolan with Elton John at the* Born to Boogie *Premier in 1973.*

sense when the leading lights of the new wave began to pay homage to him, either in words, song or spirit. The Damned, the Buzzcocks and Siouxsie and the Banshees were as much children of Bolan's revolution as they were Iggy Pop's or the Velvet Underground's.

Young Mark Feld's schoolday thoughts of stardom began to seem infinitely more attainable the day chirpy teenage goody-goody Helen Shapiro topped the charts with 'Walking Back To Happiness'. A couple of years earlier, in 1959, the pair were members of Susie and the Hula Hoops, one of thousands of school jugbands formed in a wave of Lonnie Donegan hysteria. Mark waited a good deal longer for his recording contract to come, and in any case, he had other distractions. Obsessed with his appearance (attributable, some say, to an early reading of *The Life Of Beau Brummell*), Mark's foppishness meant he was soon in demand as a fashion model, and even led to bit parts in television series.

His soft, angelic features also won him a constant supply of female admirers, though he increasingly chose to spend his time practising the guitar and immersing himself in the mythology of Ancient Greece.

Fantasy played a large part in Marc's life and quite often obscured the more mundane realities behind certain events. The first and most endearing example of Bolan's need to create his own mythology appeared in the press release which accompanied the first 'Marc Bolan' single in 1965. 'The Wizard' was supposedly based on a character Marc had stayed with for a year while in France and who, Bolan claimed, was a Chateau-bound magician with extraordinary powers. Encountering a reasonably perceptive mortal during a three or four week stay in Paris was closer to the truth. It was a tale Marc would recount throughout his career with little regard for consistency, though always convincing in its sincerity.

Bolan has often been called an opportunist, rarely a visionary. Much of his music is obviously derivative, yet it remains totally unique and instantly recognizable as his own. Even the mild travesties recorded during his later years are nothing less than ersatz Marc Bolan. If his obvious mentors back in 1965-66 were Dylan and Donovan, it was undoubtedly Cat Stevens who reaped the success of his style a year or two later. In fact, by 1967, it seemed like the entire pop world bar Engelbert Humperdinck and Sir Francis Chichester had discovered mysticism and whimsy.

By this time, Marc's failure to find success inspired him to develop what was to be his most characteristic and potent pop weapon, his voice. The quavering, caterwauling effect rendering most of his lyrics indecipherable, was a temporary drawback for the would-be poet, though few could help but sit up and listen when he sang. Three years later, when Marc smelt success in the air, he toned down his affected vibrato, having seen what Mungo Jerry's Ray Dorset had done with the Bolan warble on 'In The Summertime'. This appropriation of a vocal style that was distinctly of his own making was undoubtedly opportunist, as was his rediscovery of the musical economy of the rock'n'roll of his youth. The fusion of both dominated British pop music for three years.

To the majority of pop fans, it seemed as if Bolan and T. Rex sprang from nowhere when 'Ride A White Swan' became a massive hit in the autumn of 1970. But after his early failures, and a brief fling with flower-power poppers John's Children in Spring 1967, Marc found an audience for his music amongst the sprouting underground. His enchanted tales were delivered in a somewhat rarified manner as he sat cross-legged on an Indian rug, furiously picking and strumming a £6 acoustic guitar, while his accompanist Steve Peregrine Took fleshed out the sound with bongos and assorted toy instruments. In spite of the seemingly humble demeanour (which he adopted after

*Marc Bolan's massive overnight success was eventually grounded by a creative lull.*

witnessing the intimacy of a Ravi Shankar concert), Marc named the duo Tyrannosaurus Rex, after the largest animal ever to walk the earth. Its enormity also provided an accurate reflection of his ambitions in the rock world.

During the three years as Tyrannosaurus Rex, Bolan became a well-known figure in British rock's Second Division, and even enjoyed a couple of minor hit singles. The duo's appeal was geared towards the album-buying public, but after four reasonably successful LPs, their popularity remained stagnant. If, by 1970, Marc's Medusa-like mop of corkscrew hair still symbolized the apex of counter-culture elegance, it was clear that audiences

had tired of the love and peace brigade's romanticism and were turning to hard rock. Bolan sensed this new mood and called upon the likes of Eric Clapton to help improve his electric guitar technique. In the meantime, Took had been replaced by Mickey Finn; and the electrified simplicity of 'Ride A White Swan' became the first record to go out under the truncated name of T. Rex.

The Golden Age of Bolan had begun, and Marc capitalized on his success by expanding the T. Rex line-up to a more conventional four-piece, and writing some of the most infectious sides of popular music since the early days of Lennon and McCartney. The titles emphasized his new-found rock'n'roll sensibility and served to create a whole new mystique around him: 'Electric

*In 1977 Marc looked to be on the threshold of a comeback with* The Marc Show, *but he died in a car crash before the six episodes were released.*

Warrior', 'Cosmic Dancer', 'Metal Guru', 'The Slider', '20th Century Boy', 'The Groover', 'Zinc Alloy'. Marc rejected his past musical achievements insisting that he'd been 'Born To Boogie' all along, that his old 'Hippy Gumbo' had been mumbo-jumbo, and lambasted those who could not accept the transformation.

One of the most notable victims was Radio One disc jockey John Peel, who'd spent much of the late sixties with Marc discussing their favourite records and travelling up and down the country in a hired red mini playing and dee-jaying to generally indifferent audiences. Tyrannosaurus Rex recorded many sessions for Peel's *Top Gear* show over a period of three years, and airtime was even found for Marc to recite his poetry. But when the

DJ decided not to play 'Get It On', the third T. Rex hit, on his show, the once close relationship came to an abrupt end.

This was not an isolated case. Marc had often come across as a particularly cocksure individual: 'I was always a star,' he once said, 'even if it was only being the star of three streets in Hackney.' The pampered lifestyle offered by the obligatory retinue of courtiers and sycophants was enthusiastically accepted by Superstar Bolan. Reality, for Marc, now resided in his own greatness and only the fawning survived in his circle. Even June Child, whom he married in February 1970, dropped out of the picture when Marc fell for Gloria Jones, a soul singer who had joined his backing band at the end of 1973, and who became the mother of Rolan Bolan two years later.

Sadly Gloria's musical influence failed to provide the answer when Marc sensed that his formula – which had given him 11 consecutive

UK Top Ten hits between 1970 and 1973 – was growing stale. In an attempt to widen his appeal and to break into the American market, Bolan expanded the T. Rex line-up to incorporate backing singers and keyboards. The funked-up results only found favour with his most faithful following and T. Rex quickly became yesterday's heroes. Never again could Bolan boast to his friend Ringo Starr, '300,000 in five days, Number One in two weeks.'

There were no more Top Ten singles but by 1977, having recorded six episodes of *The Marc Show* for television, and establishing links with the burgeoning punk movement by touring with the Damned, a rejuvenated, slimmed-down Marc Bolan looked to be on the threshold of a serious comeback. ('Comeback' was, of course, a word which existed outside Marc's vocabulary: 'There are a lot of people falling off in the pop world,' he said in 1976, 'but I'm still here'.) A fatal car crash near Barnes Common, London, in the early hours of 16 September 1977 means we will never know how sustained this apparent revival could have been.

Vaudeville as *The Marc Show* was, I don't think Bolan would have ended up performing freak shows for the punks like his glam rival Gary Glitter. He was an entertainer more than anything else, and could ham it up with the best of them, but it's difficult to imagine Marc happily resigned to being simply an object of derision. And besides, all that spit would have spoilt his make-up.

Marc was a songwriter, surely his songs would have reflected the excitement and vitality of the new wave generation. After all, most of the young protagonists were T. Rex fans who'd grown up and got guitars. He may have had his day, but the influence and admiration of the new heroes would certainly have had a positive effect on his music. As it turned out, it did.

17

# Tommy Bolin

## 1 August 1951 - 4 December 1976

### by David Fricke

*Tommy Bolin was born in Sioux City on 1 August 1951. After experimenting with drums, keyboard and guitar from an early age, Bolin concentrated on guitar and played with several small bands (Benny and the Triumphs, American Standard, Zephyr) before forming his own band Energy, at the end of the sixties. When this folded in 1972, he joined the James Gang, subsequently leaving to go solo. He joined Deep Purple in 1975, replacing Ritchie Blackmore on guitar. A prolific composer, Bolin wrote or co-wrote 7 out of 10 songs on his first album with Deep Purple (Come Taste The Band). However, the band suffered from his increasing dependence on heroin, the ultimate cause of his death on 4 December 1976, eight months after Deep Purple's final concert.*

The tragedy of guitarist Tommy Bolin's death on 4 December 1976 at age 25 was not its senseless cause – an overdose of drugs and alcohol – or even his extreme youth. He simply died with too much to live for, far more than your average rock'n'roll Joe could ever hope for.

He was, for example, enviably handsome in an exotic, deeply sexual way. A luxuriant carpet of thick dark brown curls draped over his shoulders, framing a broad ruggedly boyish face with the high,

gracefully sculpted cheekbones of an American Indian. Born on 1 August 1951, in Sioux City, Iowa, he had the bold imposing warrior presence of that tribe, stalking concert stages with lithe panther-like grace and firing sharp articulate riffs from his guitar with the intuitive accuracy of a champion archer. And he was also armed with a toothy radiant smile guaranteed to dissolve women into fits of schoolgirl giggles and dreamy sighs.

But Bolin did not just look like a guitar hero; he played like one,

demonstrating a precocity that impressed his own heroes – Joe Walsh, Jeff Beck, John McLaughlin, Larry Coryell. On his first album, a 1969 release entitled *Zephyr*, recorded by a Denver-based hippie blues-rock band of the same name, Bolin, then only eighteen, was already whipping off scrappy Beck-a-phonic blues licks and bristling power chords with upstart confidence and sassy flair. By the time he was called by ex-Mahavishnu Orchestra drummer Billy Cobham to play on the latter's 1973 solo debut *Spectrum*, Bolin was mature enough to negotiate the choppy rhythms and intricate fusion turns of jazz-rock while flashing his own cocky guitar smarts, shot through with hot rock passion and funky grit.

And with his chops came success. Expelled from high school in Sioux City in 1967 for refusing to cut his hair, Bolin was soon surrounded by all the easy money and easy action that goes with rock stardom at an age when most of his peers were struggling for beer money in bars. The *Spectrum* album brought him the respect of critics who heard in Bolin's playing a stylish mix-

*Bolin had an imposing warrior presence reminiscent of an American Indian.*

*Deep Purple in 1975. Left to right: Ian Paice, David Coverdale, Tommy Bolin, Glenn Hughes and Jon Lord.*

ture of jazz and Latin influences and roaring heavy metal boogie. His fellow musicians agreed. When Joe Walsh left the James Gang in 1973, he recommended Bolin as his replacement. Two James Gang albums later (*Bang* later that same year and 1974's *Miami*), Bolin got a phone call from Deep Purple, asking him to step into founding guitarist Ritchie Blackmore's newly vacant shoes.

Success, it turned out, came too fast, even for a young man of Bolin's creative ambition and roaring enthusiasm. In an interview done in early 1976, he raved to me about the Deep Purple gig, jubilant to be playing in one of rock's biggest bands on some of the world's biggest stages. 'Before, I got the impression it was really Ritchie Blackmore's band. [Bassist] Glenn Hughes wasn't even allowed on his side of the stage. But now it feels more like a band. And I can go and get my cookies off whenever I

want to.'

That did not last long. When Bolin joined Deep Purple, the band was in fact about to collapse under the weight of inflated egos and superstar ennui. The one album Bolin cut with Purple, *Come Taste The Band*, was colourless sludge, remarkable only for his fast fluent riffing and crafty song ideas, like the heavy metal stripper instrumental 'Owed To ''G'' '. In addition, Bolin tried to juggle his Purple tour commitments with his own solo recording career, which had already pro-

*Bolin in deep water – periodic drug binges and excessive drinking led to his death aged 25.*

duced an impressive debut, *Teaser*.

When Deep Purple finally crawled to a halt in mid-1976 – barely a year after Bolin joined – he bounced back with a second solo record, *Private Eyes*. But he bounced back badly. Periodic drug binges and excessive drinking were reported. One solo tour that year was allegedly cancelled because Bolin lost his voice due to his boozing. His finances were a mess; the expense of maintaining his own band (not to mention that of his chemical diversions) caused him to lose up to $10,000 a week, which even heavy tour support from his label Columbia Records could not dam up. He was also feeling the emotional strain of a painful break-up with a long-time girlfriend.

It was in 1976 that Tommy Bolin finally cracked under the pressure in Miami, Florida. Ironically, he was beaming like a schoolboy that night of 3 December; he had the honour of opening a show with his band there at the Jai-Alai Fronton for one of his guitar gods, Jeff Beck. Back at the hotel after a strong well-received set of his own, Bolin retired to his hotel room early the next morning with two friends to discuss a business venture. When Bolin passed out in his room shortly afterwards, the friends called members of his road crew and later a doctor to check him out. But then he was put into bed to rest. A Bolin roadie claimed in one published report that he didn't call an ambulance because he thought it was a false alarm and the attention would have brought bad publicity to the band. At about seven am on the morning of 4 December, Tommy Bolin died of suffocation caused by a muscular arrest brought on by an overdose of heroin, alcohol, cocaine and barbiturates.

Among top rock guitarists, Bolin was no original in the fashion of Beck, Clapton or Bloomfield, but he was an imaginative, classy technician with big boogie balls and enormous drive. It was that drive that finally killed him. 'The only person who could tell Tommy to cool it,' his old girlfriend Karen Ulibarri told *Rolling Stone* after his death, 'was Tommy.'

# John Bonham

## 31 May 1948 - 25 September 1980

## by David Fricke

*John Bonham was born in Redditch, Worcestershire on 31 May 1948. He played drums in a Birmingham-based group Band of Joy with Robert Plant before both went on to join the New Yardbirds in 1968. Their first tour in Scandinavia was followed by a change of name to Led Zeppelin and an unsuccessful tour of the UK circuit. The group decided to concentrate on the US market and through touring and the release of their first album in 1968 they gained a reputation for sophisticated, high energy rock. Careful regulation of tours and album releases ensured a reputation as possibly the best live attraction in rock music. Bonham died on 25 September 1980 from asphyxiation after a heavy drinking session.*

If success always has its price, then for all their millions and world-wide fame Led Zeppelin certainly paid through the nose. Whether that tragic rate of exchange had anything to do with leader-guitarist Jimmy Page's alleged tampering with the occult is still a matter of hushed speculation. But there is no question that Zeppelin's karma came in a chilling shade of black. In 1975, singer Robert Plant and his wife were involved in a near-fatal car accident on the Greek island of Rhodes. Plant's five-year-old son

Karac was not so lucky when, two years later, he went down with a mysterious viral infection and suddenly died. Plant immediately flew home to England grief-stricken, prematurely ending a U.S. concert tour already plagued by ill fortune. Earlier in that tour while in San Francisco, manager Peter Grant, drummer John Bonham and two Zeppelin crew heavies allegedly ganged up on and severely beat an employee of concert promoter Bill Graham after he supposedly roughed up Grant's young son.

But even Zeppelin – the Sherman tank of rock'n'roll, a group whose fearsome cast-iron blues rock set the precedent for heavy metal music in the 1970s – never recovered from the sudden death of John Bonham, 32, on 25 September 1980, just before an American tour. The four members of Led Zeppelin (Page, Plant, Bonham and bassist John Paul Jones) were gathered at Jimmy Page's imperial Windsor estate, 25 miles outside London, on the evening of 24 September for tour rehearsals. Bonham, who was forced to cancel a show on the group's recent European tour due to physical exhaustion, had been drinking heavily that evening. John Paul Jones finally helped Bonham up to bed shortly after midnight. When he checked on Bonham the next afternoon, the drummer was dead.

If Bonham's death came as a crippling shock to the band, who were then riding high on the release of their first studio LP in four years, *In Through The Out Door*, the cause of it was cruelly predictable. He was asphyxiated by his own vomit after

*When Jimmy Page recruited him to Led Zeppelin in 1968, Bonham was a thoroughly accomplished drummer.*

*Bonham's heavy drinking and outrageous behaviour earned him the nickname 'The Beast'.*

reportedly drinking 40 measures of vodka in a twelve-hour binge; not unexpected behaviour for someone who played fifteen-minute drum solos on stage with his bare hands and smashed enough cars and hotel rooms to be nicknamed 'The Beast'. In his fantasy sequence in the Zeppelin concert film *The Song Remains The Same*, he was pictured as a Formula I racing car driver speeding like a demon down English country lanes on a motorcycle (without a sissy helmet, naturally) to the rockslide sound of his 'look, ma, no sticks' solo, 'Moby Dick'.

Still, it was John Henry Bonham's brute strength and complete disregard for politeness and subtlety that made him Jimmy Page's dream drummer when the latter was forming a new band after the Yardbirds' last gasp in 1968. Ironically, Page's first choice for his new band's drum seat had been the far more tasteful B.J. Wilson, a heavy but stylish hitter who put the sharp rock crack in Procol Harum's more baroque pop gestures. It was Robert Plant – a 20-year-old blond bluesy belter recommended to Page by singer Terry Reid – who suggested Bonham, a co-member of a respected Birmingham outfit called Band of Joy.

Born 31 May 1948 in Redditch, Worcestershire, Bonham (later known as 'Bonzo' to both friends and fans) was already a veteran of tough R&B club bands on the rowdy Birmingham circuit, among them such long-forgotten sensations as Terry and the Spiders, Steve Brett and the Mavericks and the Way of Life. Before turning twenty, he toured behind American folkie Tim Rose and had turned down backing gigs with Joe Cocker and legendary British blue-eyed soul roarer Chris Farlowe. By the time Page recruited him for the future Led Zeppelin, Bonham was a thoroughly accomplished drummer with a lumbering dexterity underlined by a savage

backbeat, a caveman cross between Keith Moon's octopus banging and Ringo Starr's simple metronome-like slam. With the release of the Atlantic debut *Led Zeppelin* at the tail end of 1968, the rock world discovered, quite simply, its heaviest hitter.

'If it moves, I hit it. If it doesn't move, I still hit it,' was his own motto, and with each succeeding Zeppelin album and tour, he always lived up to it. On *Led Zeppelin*, recorded in a breathless 30 hours, Bonham introduced himself on the opening salvo, 'Good Times Bad Times', with a fat double wallop on the tom-toms and a fast hard drum roll across the kit that sounded like a ten-car collision. He opened 'Rock And Roll', the amphetamine Chuck Berry stormer on the group's fourth album (the one with the ZOFO-style runes in the title), with a nuclear explosion of snare drum shake, metallic cymbal rattle and bass drum boom that could be con-

sidered the original Memorex test.

But for all his inarguable muscle – and one definitely did not argue with Bonham about much – he was no percussion genius. Jimmy Page and manager Peter Grant envisioned the original Led Zeppelin as a megaband that would pick up in the stadium white-blues-rock sweepstakes where the late Cream left off. Bonham, however, was no Ginger Baker. He shared Baker's penchant for overkill drum solos but had none of his jazzy fluency or polyrhythmic agility. Bonham's signature 'Moby Dick' solo was a noisier, blustery variation on Baker's old 'Toad' blowouts, with crashing cymbals and savage snare attacks broken up by jungle boogie rumbles and bass pedal foot stomping. Spectacular in its big arena echo, undeniably physical with Bonham going at his massive kit with hard granite fists, 'Moby Dick' was rock drumming's answer to a bar-room brawl.

'Bonzo's Montreux', a studio percussion extravaganza produced by Page in Switzerland in 1975 (and

included on the group's sayonara compilation *Coda*) was more interesting, an earthquake super-overdub workout with strategic electronic treatments by Page. But Bonham's unrelentingly heavy hands reduce the piece only to promising rubble. For Bonham, anything worth doing – a drum solo, demolishing a hotel room and tragically, drinking – was worth overdoing.

That, however, is not to sell John Bonham short. He made up for his modest artistic gifts with a brute enthusiasm for hitting things that made him *the* heavy metal drummer in rock. Within the structure of Jimmy Page's Gothic blues riff stylings, keeping a firm rein on Robert Plant's sandpaper-on-tonsil wails, Bonham slammed home a larger-than-life beat that elevated Led Zeppelin's strutting cock-rock and mystical 'Stairway To Heaven' fantasies to an awesome rock'n'roll spectacle. In the end, that proved to be his undoing; he died trying to be as superhuman as the sound he made.

# Eddie Cochran

## 3 October 1938 - 17 April 1960

## by John Collis

*Eddie Cochran was born in Albert Lea, Minnesota on 3 October 1938. He learned to play guitar as a child and moved to Los Angeles when he was 15, where he formed his first group. Influenced by Elvis, Eddie moved from hillbilly to rock'n'roll, and after early recordings of teenage crooning songs he had his first rock'n'roll hit in 1958, followed by tours of the USA and Australia. In the spring of 1960 he and Gene Vincent came to Britain for a national tour, but on 17 April he was killed in a car crash near Chippenham, Wiltshire en route to Heathrow Airport.*

One fact has remained constant for 30 years: a performer's appeal relies as much on image as on sound. This image is created partly by physical appearance and clothes, and partly by a mysterious aura of real or cultivated personality surrounding the artist. For the male singer, the required look has by now covered every base, from the bull-necked machismo of Guy Mitchell to the cunning androgyny of early-seventies Bowie, with out-and-out transvesticism occasionally thrown in for gimmick effect.

Whatever the demands of the current market-place, it is somehow hard to imagine Eddie Cochran applying the eye-liner and climb-

ing into a nice cotton frock. On the other hand, he never came on as a truck-driver, not even one who chooses to suck on a chocolate bar. He was a creation of his time – a brief couple of years in the late fifties – and if you looked carefully at the mould, you could just make out the words 'James Dean'.

It would be unfair to both men to make too much of this connection, so let's be unfair for a moment. They were similarly handsome, in a way slightly at odds with the par for the times – there was an apparent

chink of vulnerability. It was this that helped them both, in turn, to be adopted as fantasy spokesmen by an emerging generation. I have just consulted a 1955 dictionary; the word 'teenager' scrapes into the addenda – by the next edition, it had become a fully-fledged word. In the image-conscious and backward-looking eighties, it's no coincidence that both men have been used by the advertising world to promote goods and services at that self-same market, but it is significant that Cochran is the one chosen to market blue jeans, the eternal teenage emblem, while Dean (incongruously) sells banking.

Dean, with his heroic taciturnity, Cochran with his 'untamed youth' (the title of the only movie in which he was allowed a substantial contribution) – were prototype 'teen idols'. Ironically, one of the chief symbols of the new adolescent freedom – the automobile – ensured that their image would never be tainted by a paunch or a receding hairline. As if by marketing strategy, they were hastily whipped off to teenage heaven so that their slim output – three movies and a handful

*With his good looks and wildcat image, Cochran became the perfect fifties' heart-throb.*

of hit records – could be preserved in aspic and recycled to succeeding generations. And, before we abandon these comparisons, we should note that they were both prodigiously talented, far in advance of the requirements of evanescent teenybop fodder. Cochran was first and foremost a musician, just as Dean was an actor.

By the time Cochran emerged as a candidate for stardom, the term 'rock'n'roll' had long changed its meaning: at first a sexual euphemism in blues lyrics, it had become the catch-all title for the music of the fifties; a fusion of the black rhythm and blues mainstream, white hillbilly, white entrepreneurial (and exploitative) skill, and youthful pocket money.

It was black performers – notably Fats Domino, Little Richard and Chuck Berry – who continued to stress that the music was nurtured by its R&B roots; but, given a lingering climate of racism, it was inevitably the two white artists, Bill Haley and Elvis Presley who marked its progressive transformation into a mass-market teenage phenomenon.

The 'regulation issue' white rock 'n'roller came from poor, rural, Southern stock, and learnt to play the guitar from an elderly black neighbour. Dirt-farmers, sharecroppers, 'working for the man', both blacks and whites in this environment were on the bottom rung of the economic ladder, but the white kids would be inculcated with their one tattered assumption of superiority – their skin colour. For those who were later to take the rock'n'roll escape route, the first sign of rebellion would be to start messing with the taboo excitement of black music. Although hillbilly grew from Celtic roots in the enclosed world of the Appalachian

*Cochran came from rural, southern stock and learnt guitar from an elderly black neighbour.*

Mountains, once it began to spread across the continent – from its first star Jimmie Rodgers on – it invariably betrayed the subtle influence of the blues.

Eddie Cochran was one of the first to show a divergence from this cotton-field pattern; he stands half-way between it and the later teen-idol model who rolled off the conveyor belts in Philadelphia and New York. 'You ain't gonna make no cotton-picker out of me,' he sang in 'Untamed Youth': the implication was correct – he'd never been one in the first place. But neither did he grow up on the mean streets.

His parents, Frank and Alice Cochrane, moved north from Oklahoma City before he was born, though he claimed in his adaptation of 'Bo Weevil' to be 'a guitar-picker from Oklahoma City'. Albert Lea, inside the southern border of Minnesota, was his birthplace, on 3 October 1938. Edward Ray was Frank and Alice's fifth child, and by the age of twelve his musical interests had finally led him to the guitar.

In 1953 the family was on the move again, travelling west to the Los Angeles suburb of Bell Gardens. A fortuitous move – Cochran, already a skilled guitarist, found himself in the West Coast centre of the record industry. If his father had decided to remain in the comparative isolation of Minnesota, Eddie could still be suffering from the summertime blues, but we probably would never have heard about it.

Cochran only stayed at school in Bell Gardens long enough to make the first of a series of musical contacts; he formed his first group with bass-playing classmate Connie 'Guybo' Smith, who remained with him into the recording years.

Eddie left school in 1954, and teamed up with the unrelated Hank Cochran; they became the nucleus of a hillbilly band calling itself, not

*Eddie Cochran in classic rock'n'roll pose in the film* The Girl Can't Help It.

surprisingly, the Cochran Brothers. Hank was only a couple of years older than Eddie, a little young to be set in his ways, but nevertheless he was to prove either unwilling or unable to adapt to the tidal wave of rock'n'roll.

At this time Eddie Cochran showed two similarities to another ambitious teenager growing up almost a thousand miles to the east. The first was a trivial coincidence: Edward Cochrane became Eddie Cochran, and Charles 'Buddy' Holley was soon to become Buddy Holly. In the first case the abandoning of the 'e' was pre-

sumably to fall in line with Hank Cochran; in Holly's case, legend puts it down to a spelling mistake.

The second similarity was more significant, stressing that the revolution caused by Presley's wild stage act took a while before it affected the second generation of rock'n'rollers (as soon as Cochran and Holly *saw* Elvis, they were changed men). In the early fifties Holly and Cochran's routes into music were both as part of hillbilly duos. Although it was some time since Bill Haley had set the ball rolling, it was to take the younger, sexier, uninhibited Presley to show the exciting way forward.

By the end of 1954 the Cochrans,

with Eddie as junior partner, had built up a local following through live and radio gigging, and had signed with the Nashville label, Ekko. Eddie's versatile skill on guitar was also leading to more and more bookings as a session player. The Cochrans' first two record releases were straight hillbilly, with Hank dominating and Eddie contributing guitar breaks and harmonies. But then two important things happened to Eddie: he saw Elvis for the first time when the Cochrans were lower down a concert bill in Dallas, and he met Jerry Capehart in a Bell Gardens music store. Capehart became his manager, mentor and songwriting partner.

The third single by the Cochrans showed that the collaboration couldn't last much longer. 'Tired And Sleepy' and 'Fool's Paradise', in particular the latter, took strides away from hillbilly towards rock 'n'roll, with Eddie now as the more prominent contributor.

By now Eddie, Jerry and 'Guybo' had built up a little portfolio of records and demos with which to push Eddie as a rock'n'roller, including early versions of two Cochran classics, 'Skinny Jim' and 'Pink Pegged Slacks', ad-lib covers of 'Long Tall Sally' and 'Blue Suede Shoes', and – vitally – a demo of 'Twenty Flight Rock'. In turn these secured him a publishing deal, and then a record contract with Liberty. Although he was still an unknown, Liberty got him into the movie 'The Girl Can't Help It', singing a cameo of 'Twenty Flight Rock'.

After that, the rest should have been history. But Liberty didn't capitalize on the film by using 'Twenty Flight Rock' as Cochran's first release. In fact, they persistently ignored it, and for a while they seemed to be vindicated in seeing Cochran instead as a purveyor of teenage smooch novelties. 'Sittin' In The Balcony' made

*Eddie's musical roots were steeped in hillbilly but he was always a rock'n'roller at heart.*

the Top Twenty, but the slightly tougher 'Mean When I'm Mad' missed out completely; the sing-along ditty 'Drive-In Show' was a modest hit, but his first gloves-off rocker 'Jeanie Jeanie Jeanie' only limped into the Hot Hundred for a week. Cochran must have felt that he *was* a rock'n'roller at heart, but his only real success had been as a lightweight crooner.

At this stage, in the words of Jerry Capehart, 'we badly needed a hit'. So, in the course of half an hour, they fiddled about with a simple guitar riff that Cochran had devised, and came up with

'Summertime Blues'. It was *the* hit of summer 1958, his first top-tenner, and the one that broke through in Britain. Cochran toured Australia, at that time the other 'big market' outside the States, with Holly, Little Richard and Gene Vincent; he followed 'Summertime Blues' with 'C'mon Everybody', and spent a year consolidating his success at home. Then, in the spring of 1960, a year after the death of Buddy Holly, he and Gene Vincent arrived for a national tour of Britain.

Ever since the publicity machinery of *The Daily Mirror* had got behind Bill Haley in February 1957, turning his tour into a headline-grabbing regal progress around the country, visits to Britain by top

American rock'n'rollers had been something of an event. Britain had its own counterfeit models – some of them, like Cliff Richard and Billy Fury, highly talented performers – but even the least perceptive of the fans must have known that it was an American form of music, and that the originals couldn't be beaten.

Eddie Cochran, for his charm and wit in interviews as well as for his talent; Gene Vincent, a neurotic dressed in black leather by impresario Jack Good; Buddy Holly, whose 1958 tour had inspired a generation of British guitarists – all remained heroes and substantial record-sellers in the UK long after they had been moved to the 'nostalgia bin' at home. And since Cochran died on British soil – in a car crash en route to Heathrow on 17 April 1960, after completing his UK tour with Gene Vincent – he was swiftly elevated to sainthood in the hearts of British rock'n'roll fans. The release at the time of his death, ironically entitled 'Three Steps To Heaven', was a massive hit, and his recordings have been continuously re-packaged and recycled ever since.

Although these releases stressed the breadth of Cochran's short-lived talent – at one extreme he could wring a harshly-convincing blues from his guitar, at the other croon seductively through a knee-quivering teen ballad – it was as spokesman for his generation that his image gets its final, vital gloss. The frustrations and excitements of adolescence, the brick wall formed by disapproving ranks of parents, teachers and employers, the yearning for a car and 'my own private phone' – Eddie Cochran summed up this 1950s battleground like no one else. And his death will forever protect this image from the sober qualifications of middle age.

*'Summertime Blues' was the song that really launched Cochran in 1958.*

# Sam Cooke

## 22 January 1931 - 11 December 1964

## by Cliff White

*Sam Cooke was born in Clarksdale, Mississippi on 22 January 1931. He sang gospel from an early age, and joined leading group the Soul Stirrers in 1951, leaving in 1956 when he moved across into rhythm'n'blues. His first single, 'You Send Me', was released in 1957, reaching Number 1 in both R&B and pop charts. In 1958 Cooke signed to a major label, RCA, and began to assume total artistic control of his record output. Between 1960 and 1964 he and his manager operated their own independent label, encouraging further black talent. On 11 December 1964 Sam Cooke was shot dead in a motel room in rather unsavoury circumstances.*

If it was only for his exemplary singing style and for many of the songs he wrote during his abruptly curtailed career as a popular entertainer, Sam Cooke would still be a prominent name among the Late Greats. Let the records speak for themselves: an almost unbroken run of American hits, comprising 43 entries in the Pop Hot 100, nine of them posthumous, and 29 entries in the rhythm'n'blues Top 40, five of them posthumous. Most of the hits were self-composed; several were also international hits; many are still being regularly revived by other singers; all add up to a sub-stantial legacy of sublimely sung and, for the most part, well-crafted performances of considerable influence. But Cooke was more than just a gifted singer and songsmith. Although his voice was his premier asset, and seldom better showcased than by his own songs, his ultimate importance had as much to do with the pioneering course of his career through the confused social and musical values of the fifties and early sixties, from which he emerged as one of the major inspirational figures in the development of soul music and the beginnings of racial realignment in the music industry.

Closely though never precisely reflecting the societies in which they operate, the American and British music industries are still far more partitioned than they profess to be. It is still true, for example, that the vast majority of record companies, distribution channels, retail stores and media outlets of both countries are controlled and predominantly staffed by whites. Likewise, although no longer quite so disproportionately omnipotent, a large majority of the 'stars' fostered by the industries are white, even though most of the fundamentally important post-war music changes can be directly or indirectly traced to blacks, particularly to black America.

For all that, it is equally true that there have been substantial changes in western societies and their music industries over the last two or three decades. Changes enough so that today, in the eighties, it might seem incredible to new generations that only 25 years ago it was still an extraordinary achievement for any

*Sam Cooke began his career as lead singer of the gospel group, the Soul Stirrers.*

black recording artist to break up and through the racial barrier to impinge on the dominant white market. And it was then against all the odds for such an artist to consolidate the achievement by assuming artistic control of his (or, of course, her) own career and financial control of his own song publishing rights, on the side establishing a flourishing independent recording/production company, all the time increasing in general popularity while gradually moving *away* from the vacuous norms of pop towards a more satisfying expression of personal roots. Sam Cooke pioneered just such a course.

Even well into the sixties, after Cooke's death, by which time records by black artists were more regularly hitting the pop charts, few of the artists themselves were yet exposed and promoted to the general public in the same way that white recording artists were. While the post-rock'n'roll pop industry was blossoming into an internationally newsworthy phenomenon, turning hordes of white adolescents into instant personalities, most black artists remained faceless names on record labels, of no personal account except to their original black audiences. Under the circumstances, then, it is one measure of Sam Cooke's special status – albeit the most morbid and least important measure – that his death on 11 December 1964 was widely reported by the western media, including the front pages of some British daily newspapers. To be sure his death got bigger coverage than it might have done because it was, or was reported to be, a particularly sordid affair. He is alleged to have brought a young woman back to a motel room against her will after a Los Angeles party. After a long scuffle, the woman managed to escape to call the police from a nearby phone box. Cooke, now incensed with fury and dressed in

*Cooke was hailed as the black Renaissance Man and a symbol of hope for his generation.*

no more than a raincoat, ran down to the manager's office and broke down the door, demanding to know where the woman had disappeared to. A violent argument ensued which ended in Cooke assaulting the manager, who finally pulled a gun and shot him three times at close range. However, the very fact that it all made such good copy was ironic acknowledgement of his status.

At the same time, a greater measure of Cooke's status could be assessed from what *wasn't* widely reported by the western media: that in the days following his death, while his body lay in state in Chicago and then Los Angeles, an estimated total of 200,000 people filed past the casket in tribute to

the singer; that funeral ceremonies in both cities were chaotically over-attended scenes of mass grief and hysteria; and that the whole drama culminated in a 200-car procession from the L.A. church to the burial site. This wasn't simply a case of 'Negro Pop Star Shot Dead in L.A. Motel'; this was communal distress at the sudden incongruous wasting of a major black talent.

Born in Clarksdale, Mississippi on 22 January 1931, Sam was one of seven children to Anna Mae and Charles Cooke. Shortly after his birth the family migrated up to Chicago's South Side, where his father became a preacher in the Baptist Church of Christ Holiness. Sam was soon singing in the choir of the church and by the ripe old age of nine was fronting a gospel quartet, the Singing Children, accompanied by a brother and two sisters. There was nothing particularly unusual in this. The majority of American performers from southern-rooted families, black and white, first sang or played as children in a Baptist or similarly evangelical church. But whereas most got sidetracked into more secular pursuits during their teens, Sam stayed 'with God' rather longer. He didn't, however, stay as long as was expected of him by the rest of black gospel-motivated society. Both events – his initial pursuit of gospel music and his eventual switch to secular music – turned out to be critical stages in his career.

While still in high school, Sam was asked to lead the newly formed Highway QCs, a group organized as a sort of junior league adjunct to one of the top gospel teams of the day, the Soul Stirrers.

Gospel differed from older forms of religious singing in content (mainly new songs instead of traditional Christian hymns and Spirituals) but especially in style: formal vocal arrangements were replaced by adventurous improvization, shifting rhythm and harmony patterns, and a greater emphasis on lead singers of exhilarating vocal dexterity. Formed in 1935, the Soul Stirrers were among the first and greatest of the new breed of gospel groups, with lead singer Robert (R.H.) Harris perhaps the most revered and influential stylist of his generation. When Harris left the Soul Stirrers, 20-year-old Sam Cooke was moved up a league to replace him in January 1951.

The transfer was a colossal risk for the Soul Stirrers, for although Cooke had equipped himself admirably in the junior league, on the main stage of the gospel scene he was an unknown kid stepping into the shoes of a great star. He wore them so well that even his first appearances and recordings with the group were successfully received; better still, it wasn't long

before he'd totally eclipsed old memories of the group, leading the Soul Stirrers to greater success than ever before with himself becoming the first pop-style idol and sex symbol of gospel music, attracting hordes of swooning teenage girls wherever he performed. All the more remarkable, he achieved all this without indulging in the histrionic exhibitionism by then favoured by so many other gospel singers.

Cooke was a livelier, hipper personality and singer than Harris but he retained much of the dignified style of his predecessor and was just as seriously involved in the music and message of gospel. Over the six years that he led the Soul Stirrers he wrote many memorable songs for the group, including 'Nearer To Thee', 'Be With Me Jesus', and their biggest ever hit, 'Touch The Hem Of His Garment'. Nevertheless, by the mid-fifties his popularity was getting too great to be contained by the gospel circuit, especially as his most vociferous fans were of the new young generation that no longer cut clear divisions between 'good' gospel music and 'bad' popular music; indeed, most of them were probably sneaking R&B records into the house when they weren't attending Soul Stirrers concerts to see Sam. Not only that, the group's record company, Specialty, had just hit international paydirt with Little Richard (a lot of whose manic style was an idiosyncratic exaggeration of gospel music) and other record companies were starting to make lucrative offers for Sam. The result was almost inevitable; firmly encouraged by his friend and mentor J. W. Alexander (himself an ex-gospel singer turned manager/producer), in 1956 Cooke finally plunged into the big bad world of secular music.

By then a lot of the most popular black rhythm'n'blues acts had come from gospel-singing backgrounds (Clyde McPhatter, for instance) or

were freely borrowing musical ideas from gospel (Ray Charles); several were in their own ways as stylistically influential as Cooke. But Sam was the first major, established, honest to God gospel star – and the hottest of the day, at that – to go pop; it was a fateful decision. The more reactionary members of the gospel community never forgave him for turning to 'the Devil's music', some even seeing his premature death as divine retribution. To most, though, especially his own generation, his switch and subsequent success was as inspirational as his singing style.

Initially, Specialty Records' boss Art Rupe was dead set against the star of his best-selling gospel group risking a pop release. Finally persuaded, his worst fears seemed realized when Sam's first pop single (credited to 'Dale Cook' in a vain attempt to disguise the singer's identity) did nothing much except provoke rumblings of disquiet in the gospel market. When Rupe sat on the proposed follow-up release, producer Bumps Blackwell bought Sam's contract and some of his other unissued tracks, eventually placing them with another L.A. company, Keen. From those tracks, 'You Send Me', a lightweight but exquisitely performed ballad, hit Number 1 on both the R&B and pop charts in October 1957, reputedly selling around $2^{1/2}$ million copies.

On the strength of the breakthrough Cooke left the Soul Stirrers, Blackwell took over as manager, and the quest for fame and fortune began in earnest. Unfortunately there were no new maps available to either destination; the repercussions of the rock'n'roll boom had yet to penetrate the main body of the music industry.

For any black artist competing in such a climate the options were even less enticing. You could take your chances in the pop market, providing you realized that you

were no more welcome than the crudest of white rockers, even if you were clean cut, apparently wholesome and comparatively free of unseemly 'nigger' mannerisms. But if you had all that going for you, could hoof it a bit, and were prepared to smile a lot and sing all the right songs, there might be a place for you as entertainer to the white bourgeoisie. Providing, of course, that you kept your nose clean, did what you were told, and bore in mind that 'safe' and internationally respected black entertainers like Nat 'King' Cole and Sammy Davis Jnr often still couldn't eat or sleep in the establishments where they were booked to entertain, and, as happened to Cole in 1956, none was immune from physical attack on stage by a bunch of southern white crackers. All in all, black boy, you were best advised to keep your head down and stick with your own kind.

Over the next three years Sam trod an uncharted and at times uncomfortable path between all three options, surviving not so much by canny strategy but perhaps more because he was not extreme in any one style, nor, at that time, extremely successful with any one audience. Without venturing beyond light, catchy tunes on single releases he retained middle-weight popularity in both the black R&B and white pop markets, his best remembered Keen hits including 'Win Your Love For Me', 'Everybody Likes To Cha Cha Cha', 'Only Sixteen' and 'Wonderful World'.

If the singles were less adventurous than his talent deserved, at least the best of them had a lot of charm. Not so his albums. Mainly comprising lamely orchestrated showbiz standards, they reflected Sam's disastrous slide towards the artistically stupefying

*Cooke influenced many later artists but few could match the compelling beauty of his voice.*

supper club circuit. Fortunately his first appearance at the Copacabana in 1958 was poorly attended and critically slated, otherwise he might have got sucked into the syndrome early in his pop career. As it was he remained to some extent associated with the tuxedo brigade until the end, and was recorded on a more successful return to the Copa only six months before his death. It was his renewed association with Alexander that sparked off that important last phase of his career.

In 1958, while Cooke still recorded for Keen, Alexander had started his own song publishing company, Kags Music; he soon brought Sam in as a partner and became his manager. The following year they sued Keen for default on royalty payments and negotiated a much stronger recording deal with the major RCA corporation, where they were placed with the white producers known collectively as 'Hugo & Luigi'.

The producers' ideas for Sam were no more imaginative than Blackwell's earlier efforts, resulting in a couple of tepid teen-ballad singles and an album of cabaret standards that launched Cooke's RCA career with a dull thud. Thereafter, although Hugo & Luigi's logo adorned every release, Sam and J.W. assumed control of all single issues (and eventually albums, too), generally working with black arranger Rene Hall. The trio's first collaboration yielded 'Chain Gang', which, while deliberately stylized for mass appeal, was Sam's first distinctly 'black' record since his days as a gospel singer. An international hit in September 1960, it launched four solid years of soulfully conceived productions, both carefree in content and emotionally more intense.

Over the same 1960-64 period Cooke and Alexander successfully operated their own independent record company, Sar (to which

they latterly added a second label, Derby), developing and encouraging an impressive roster of black acts, most of them produced by Cooke and frequently using his songs. Although rarely seen outside of the R&B market and charts, many of the Sar/Derby releases were excellent. More significantly, the whole set-up, also incorporating their Mallory Management agency, was an important creative addition to the small number of black-owned record operations, giving a first break to numerous talents. Some went down with the company after Cooke's death (the Sims Twins, Johnny Morisette), but others went on to become major soul stars (Billy Preston, Johnnie Taylor, Bobby Womack).

Sam Cooke wasn't the only idolized and influential black singer of his era, far from it. And neither was Sam the first black artist of his generation to break through to a mass audience. Rock'n'rollers Little Richard, Chuck Berry and Fats Domino cut different swathes before him, while many other acts scored 'crossover' hits before or about the same time as he did, without sustaining or building on that success. Nor was Sam the first to control, in partnership, publishing and production/recording concerns or to be involved in his own and other artists' management. But he was the first to be and do *all* of this, and hold it all together with an agile grace that entranced white audiences and inspired his own and subsequent generations of black artists.

To list all of the artists who owe something to Cooke's influence, either stylistically or spiritually, would be like indexing a history of 20 years of soul music. Just a critical selection of the more obvious examples would have to include, in no special order, Al Green, Otis Redding, Arthur Conley, Marvin Gaye, Aretha Franklin, the Staple

Singers, the Ovations, Lou Rawls, Johnny Nash, Joe Simon, Charles Jackson and the alumni from the Sar/Derby labels. Also, across the tracks in Rock City countless artists have been inspired by Cooke's recordings, particularly Rod Stewart, though neither he nor any other white singer has yet come close to equalling the compelling beauty of Sam's voice.

During the last few years of his life Sam Cooke had matured into an accomplished and versatile performer, equally at ease with all manner of different audiences, on stage and on his increasingly frequent TV appearances. His records were sounding and selling better than ever, not just the singles but, from 1962 on, his studio albums were consistently good too, whether gimmicky (*Twistin' The Night Away*, 1962 which was opportunistic, but still one of the best Twist albums), different shades of blue (*Mr Soul* and *Night Beat*, both 1963) or straight pop-soul with subtle indications of changing times (*Ain't That Good News*, 1964). His private life was a bit of a mess but his business interests were stable and he was beginning to explore new avenues of achievement, including a successful Hollywood screen test at which he gave a convincing reading from part of Sidney Poitier's script in *In The Heat Of The Night*. In short he was black renaissance man, a symbol of hope for his generation. Yet two months after his film test he was shot dead, apparently in circumstances that were sordid enough in themselves but seemed even more tragic because of what he represented.

In the year that he was fatally shot Sam Cooke recorded one of his most memorable songs, perhaps his most fitting valediction: 'A Change Is Gonna Come'. He didn't live to appreciate fully how right he was but he certainly helped towards setting the change in motion.

# Ian Curtis

## 15 July 1956 - 18 May 1980

## by Brian Edge

*Ian Curtis was born in Macclesfield, Cheshire on 15 July 1956. In 1977, with schoolfriends Peter Hook and Bernard Albrecht, with himself as singer and lyricist, he formed the band Warsaw. The band changed its name to Joy Division in 1978, and signed up with Manchester-based Factory Records. The following year the band produced its first album* Unknown Pleasures *which received much acclaim for its powerful lyrics and its haunting rhythms. Amid a growing reputation as the apotheosis of New Wave music, Joy Division were planning an American tour and were close to releasing their second album* Closer *when Curtis, bowed down by increasing bouts of epilepsy and a failed marriage, hanged himself on 18 May 1980.*

Towards the end of rock's most troubled decade, a band emerged in Manchester whose music promised a new beginning. Unique amongst their contemporaries, Joy Division's vivid soundscapes opened a window on the soul, signalling an end to the sneering and posing of what the Fall's Mark E. Smith fondly termed 'the '77 shit-pile'. Fused to a punishing sound and inverted rhythms, the words of singer Ian Curtis were as far removed from

punk doggerel as the Sex Pistols' wanton vulgarity had been from the frivolous world of mid-seventies pop. Unexpectedly breaking away from their coarse, unremarkable roots when they performed as Warsaw, Joy Division made the first genuine moves towards a harder, more demanding future for what had been dubbed alternative culture. Their awesome transformation from archetypal three-chord desperados to New Wave frontiersmen entranced both audiences and the music press alike. At the hour of

their demise in May 1980, with the death of Ian Curtis, Joy Division had become one of the most revered names in rock.

Joy Division consisted of four young men. Peter Hook, Stephen Morris, Bernard Dicken (who at the time preferred the pseudonym Albrecht) and Ian Curtis were equal parts of an indivisible whole, friends. Ian Curtis, who knew bass player Peter Hook and guitarist Bernard Albrecht from their days together at Salford Grammar School, formed the group's core. Drummer Stephen Morris, who hailed from Curtis's home town of Macclesfield, was only recruited at the eleventh hour, when Curtis invited him to join in time for the band's first gig.

A long and frustrated apprenticeship ended when they teamed up with newly-formed Factory Records, contributing two songs to the Manchester company's first release, *A Factory Sampler*, which appeared on Christmas Eve 1978. 'Digital', and more especially 'Glass', shamed the band's 'home-made' EP 'An Ideal For Living' released

*Curtis's stage act was passionate and anguished making him Joy Division's most charismatic figure.*

*As lyricist for the band, Ian poured out his feelings of isolation and despair in his songs.*

the previous year. Working with producer Martin Hannett, Joy Division were able to articulate their formerly conventional sound; only now did Ian Curtis begin to communicate his ideas, his images being underscored by Hannett's use of disturbing subliminal noises. The group's close relationship with Hannett and their continued involvement with Factory culminated in the release of Joy Division's first LP in June 1979. Factory boss Tony Wilson risked his life savings to finance the project, a great leap of faith that produced the debut album *Unknown Pleasures*, a fragile synthesis of power and melancholy, which earned rapturous reviews from both fanzines and the established weeklies. For Joy Division's rapidly growing following, it was a chance to share more

completely in a private music rarely heard outside the intimacy of clubs in and around northern England. At the heart of this unforgiving album stood Ian Curtis, his impassioned pleading going so far down the road towards despair in a song like 'Insight' that his voice became spell-binding. That was the attraction; that candid, raw emotion. 'Guess the dreams always end,' sang Curtis. 'They don't rise up, just descend; but I don't care any more, I've lost the will to want more; I'm not afraid, not at all, I watch them all as they fall; but I remember when we were young.'

The lyrics which Ian Curtis kept in his little book weren't didactic. Songs like 'Disorder', 'Wilderness' and 'Shadowplay', whose titles alone evoked feelings of loneliness and fear, were simply personal vignettes. They were disturbing, and full of conviction: 'Directionless, so plain to see, a

loaded gun won't set you free, so you say...' ('New Dawn Fades'). Yet as *New Musical Express* writer Paul Du Noyer rightly pointed out, 'Handled with less power, skill and verisimilitude, Curtis's images and metaphors would seem almost risible.'

Curtis's apparent alienation was connected with the collective mind of a romantic youth whose love of life's absolutes was as strong in Joy Division's time as in previous generations. Those who all too readily picked up on Joy Division's sombre nature, describing them as 'gothic' and 'doomy', or dismissed them as a kind of English Doors, were missing the point entirely. *Unknown Pleasures* reflected perfectly the band's own time and the bleakness of their surroundings. Far from crooning anew in the manner of Jim Morrison, Ian Curtis belonged firmly to the atrophied culture of late 20th Century urban Britain. Curtis's imagery captured the general air of hopelessness and decay of that period far better than any of the band's left-field peers, not least because he focussed on the individual and not the mass. Joy Division were nobody's conscience.

'She's Lost Control', undoubtedly the album's most personal track, epitomized the Joy Division ethos: there are no short answers or cures. For Curtis the song was a kind of exorcism in which he dealt openly with his epileptic condition. 'She turned around and took me by the hand and said, ''I've lost control again;'' how I'll never know just why or understand, she said, ''I've lost control again;'' and she screamed out, kicking on her side and said, ''I've lost control again;'' and she seized upon the floor, I thought she'd died, she said, ''I've lost control again...'' '

Nineteenth century Russian novelist Dostoyevsky, gave this third person account of his own epileptic attacks in *The Idiot*. 'There was a moment or two,' he wrote, 'almost before the fit itself when suddenly amid the sadness, spiritual darkness and depression, his brain seemed to catch fire at brief moments, and with an extraordinary momentum his vital forces were strained to the utmost all at once. His mind and heart were flooded by a dazzling light. All his agitation, all his doubts and worries, seemed composed in a twinkling, culminating in a great calm, full of serene and harmonious joy and hope, full of understanding and the knowledge of the final cause.'

Something of this was captured during Joy Division's performances when, bathed in an eerie blue haze, Curtis would break into a violent, cathartic dance, flailing his limbs in mockery of his affliction. These were no lame histrionics. Again on camera, when Joy Division showcased the single 'Transmission' on BBC2's new wave forum 'Something Else', Curtis, with his pale, watery eyes, exuded an aura of anguish and confusion that was uneasy to watch. It contrasted starkly with the song's throbbing beat: a more perverse form of entertainment could scarcely be imagined. Those who witnessed Joy Division late in 1979 would bear this out. Audiences around the country felt more bewildered than cheated when, after an apparent seizure, Curtis would be helped off stage before the end of the set. However, on one occasion Curtis's non-appearance, except for the last two numbers, led to a near-riot, when A Certain Ratio's Simon Topping stepped in as vocalist. Unaware that Ian Curtis was ill, the crowd had reacted violently to the 'masquerade' of Simon Topping performing the vocal honours, construing it as another of Factory's increasingly tiresome antics.

*Curtis found it difficult to cope with the pressures of rock stardom.*

On form, Ian Curtis came across as swarthy and assertive, his deep voice and animated stage persona belying a quiet, polite manner offstage. 'When I met him,' recalled *Sounds* writer Dave McCullough, 'he talked in a whisper. He talked hypnotically and enchantingly about toy shops. He spun words magically, that was his gift; he poured pure silver across totally memorable phrases and related scenarios, and he managed it in songs too.'

But this picture of Ian Curtis is as unlikely to endure as the image of Joy Division indulging in boisterous dressing room lager frenzy and football talk (Curtis was a Manchester United fan) prior to their gigs. By this point in the band's history they were already cocooned in mystique, so that mention of Joy Division trivialities were hardly ever made. Such attempts to make the band seem more human, since they were often depicted as surly and incommunicative, were usually undermined by the foursome being photographed in an urban setting, or better still, framed by a few token 'dark satanic mills'. If a cult of personality did surround Ian Curtis, it really arose by default, the inevitable result of Curtis being the frontman, the only one of the four to project an image, albeit unintentionally. For this rea-

*Joy Division. Left to right: Stephen Morris, Peter Hook, Bernard Dicken and Ian Curtis.*

son perhaps more than any other, the history of Joy Division is the history of Ian Curtis.

Factory's house style served to reinforce their anonymous image, with Peter Saville's stylishly enigmatic sleeves revealing no individual credits, let alone the obligatory group shot. Joy Division and Factory Records were happy to leave flamboyant gimmickery to everyone else. It wasn't so much that they were serious, rather that they viewed the cynical manoeuvrings of the music business as grotesque and irrelevant.

Entering the new decade, Joy Division were seemingly unstoppable. Their notoriously obscure Sordide Sentimentale single of which less than 2000 were pressed, and featuring the magnificent 'Atmosphere' and 'Dead Souls',

proved that the band were continuing to break new ground. Plans for 1980 alone included a second LP, a further single, and a repeat of their recent and highly successful European tour. Ian Curtis was especially optimistic about the proposed Spring tour of America, confident that the group would prove even more popular over there than at home. They had prepared the way with a remixed version of 'She's Lost Control' for the American market.

In Britain, Joy Division's influence was at an unprecedented peak. Big names like the Cure, Echo and the Bunnymen and Bauhaus were encouraged to put meaning in their moaning, and Joy Division were plagiarized by the nation's youngsters who flattered them in a score of soundalike bands. Unfortunately, Factory went on to patronize many of these dour, affected copyists, who couldn't hold a candle to

the true architects of incandescent emotion. Yet their fascination with Joy Division's music was so understandable. Just prior to recording their second album, *Closer*, a Joy Division concert was an inspiration to behold. Predominantly new material, including 'Love Will Tear Us Apart', 'Twenty Four Hours', and 'Isolation' showed the band using synthesizers to greater effect, without lapsing into the sterile realms of techno-pop. Ian Curtis's voice, as the posthumously released *Closer* graphically demonstrated, had become an instrument, sensuous in the extreme. 'Now that I've realised how it's all gone wrong, got to find some therapy, this treatment takes too long; deep in the heart of where sympathy held sway, got to find my destiny, before it gets too late.' ('Twenty Four Hours')

Towards the end of April 1980, Joy Division recorded a promotional video for 'Love Will Tear Us Apart', a conscious move out from the underground and into the light. They were on the verge of commercial success. Everything seemed fine. Four days later, on 2 May, Joy Division gave what was to be their last performance at Birmingham University. A recording of that final concert comprised one half of the retrospective double-album *Still*, which reached Number 5 in the UK album charts.

For Ian Curtis, the pressures of life had become too great for him to bear, and in the early hours of Sunday 18 May, on the eve of their US tour, he hanged himself. He had not even reached his 24th birthday. A fragment of the note he left read, 'At this very moment I just wish I were dead. I just can't cope any more.'

He left behind a wife and child.

Those closest to Curtis had been aware of a deterioration in his mental and physical health. They also knew he was a sensitive character given to bouts of acute depression, but no one had suspected suicide, despite the fact he had made two previous attempts to take his own life. 'He was not a weird guy,' reflected Bernard Albrecht. 'He was a normal person like anyone else, that was the thing about it, but a very emotional person, and some people can show their emotions, but he didn't show his, except on rare occasions. In his lyrics...' Curtis's death was tragic in the sense that it had little in common with the squalid heroin deaths of Sid Vicious, and the Ruts' Malcolm Owen whom everyone seems to have forgotten. Appropriately, it was a shocked John Peel who announced the news to thousands of unsuspecting fans on his late night show. As a tribute he played 'Atmosphere' – 'Don't walk away in silence...'

The effect of Ian Curtis's death on Joy Division's music now seems predictable. However incorrect our

*Curtis would mimic his own epilepsy by flailing his limbs wildly on stage.*

assumptions about his suicide may be, the finality of the act has rubber-stamped Joy Division's credibility, and their work will forever be regarded in a compelling light. In the wake of all the eulogies and the apologies for past remarks about slashed wrists made in reference to Joy Division, the rock press visibly recoiled. If circumstances had been otherwise, if Ian Curtis had lived, one felt that perhaps they wouldn't

have embraced the rank hedonism of the 1980's quite so readily.

New Order, formed by Joy Division's extant members, with the addition of keyboard player/guitarist Gillian Gilbert, exploded the myth of Joy Divison and conclusively staked their claim in the modern music world with their titanic release 'Blue Monday'. Yet it is fair to say that a band of Joy Division's calibre would have occupied a similar niche, only with Ian Curtis gone, Joy Division's world is an altogether different place.

# Sandy Denny

## 6 January 1947 - 21 April 1978

## by Patrick Humphries

*Sandy Denny was born in Wimbledon, South London on 6 January 1947. After attracting attention on the folk club circuit, she joined her first group, the Strawbs in 1968, but soon left to join Fairport Convention in May that year. She made three albums with them before leaving in November 1969. In March 1970 she formed her own band, Fotheringay which folded after only a year. In 1973 after some critical and commercial success as a solo artist, she married Trevor Lucas, guitarist with Fairport, and rejoined the group in 1974. She left again in 1976 to continue her solo career. Her daughter Georgia was born in 1977, but Sandy died on 21 April 1978 after falling down a flight of stairs at a friend's house.*

When Fairport Convention get together for their once-or-twice-yearly reunion tour, the tickets at each venue sell out within 24 hours. This might not be remarkable, except that Fairport is a folk rock band originally formed in 1967, has never had a Top Ten hit and whose entry in *The NME Encyclopedia of Rock* states that 'it would be difficult to name a band that's paid more dues and been rewarded with such wretched luck'. But Fairport's fans have singular devotion and long memories – and when the band plays one of Sandy Denny's songs their audiences respond with poignant fervour.

Sandy Denny is chiefly remembered for her work with Fairport Convention, even though she did make a few creditable solo albums. Although the band had been formed by a group of young North Londoners and had originally had a female singer in the line-up, it needed a voice of Sandy's strength and purity to complement their style of playing. Born in south-west London on 6 January 1947,

Sandy began singing on the folk club circuit when she left school. Initially influenced by Americans like Tom Paxton and Jackson C. Frank, she joined the Strawbs for a while before being auditioned for Fairport Convention in 1968. 'She stood out like a clean glass in a sinkful of dirty dishes,' said Simon Nicol, a member of Fairport's original line-up.

Sandy's time with the band was when it was at its most influential. Fairport's *Liege and Lief* album (1969) virtually defined 'folk rock' and it was Sandy Denny who helped steer them in that important direction. Her musical apprenticeship in the folk clubs brought them the traditional 'A Sailor's Life', which Fairport transformed into an epochal electric jam on their *Unhalfbricking* album (also 1969), paving the way for their whole-hearted commitment to this interpretation of the traditional on *Liege and Lief.*

Yet Sandy Denny's musical scope was much wider than this early, 'folkie' image might imply. Her voice had a marvellous range – she had the ability, in Simon Nicol's

*Sandy's voice had a strength and purity which singled her out as something special.*

*Fairport Convention in 1968: Left to right: Simon Nicol, Martin Lamble, Ashley Hutchings, Richard Thompson, Sandy Denny.*

words, to get 'shades of emotion across, from moodiness to compassion to outright fury. There's not many singers can do that.' The fans agreed: she was voted Best Female Singer two years running in the annual *Melody Maker* poll, but she herself chafed at the traditionalism of Fairport's late sixties output. Her own songs drew on that tradition, but also show the influence of more modern and popular idioms. She was a moving force behind the 1972 album, *The Bunch*, in which many of the folk-rock fraternity enjoyed themselves covering rock'n'roll standards, and her haunting version of Buddy Holly's 'Learning The Game' was particularly outstanding. She even duetted with Robert Plant on the *Led Zeppelin IV* album.

Like Joni Mitchell, Sandy's own songs sprang from personal experience but were never too esoteric to be unapproachable. They were wistful songs in an English mood. On her solo albums they were aided

by the sympathetic orchestrations of Harry Robinson, who gave her songs the scope they deserved. Their most successful collaboration came with the title track of her third album, *Like An Old Fashioned Waltz* (1973). There was a lingering poignancy in her best songs, which leaves them occupying a unique place in English popular music. Her best-known song is probably 'Who Knows Where The Time Goes', a beautiful forlorn melody of romance which she recorded with Fairport Convention in 1969, and which Judy Collins covered as the title track to her eighth album.

Sandy Denny's time with Fairport Convention was tantalisingly short – but then the band was beset by splits and re-formations throughout its life. The strains of touring and separation from her husband-to-be, Trevor Lucas, plus difficulties over the musical direction in which the band was going persuaded her with regret to leave the band in 1969. In 1970 she formed her own group, Fotheringay, with Trevor Lucas and others, and recorded solo during this period, but when Trevor himself was

recruited into yet another Fairport Convention line-up it was inevitable that she should accompany them on a world tour, and equally inevitable that she should end up joining them on stage again. But it only lasted a year. The tour had been a financial disaster and in 1975 the band finally split, unable to survive the strains it put on its members' personal relationships as well as their pockets.

Sandy Denny was only 31 when she died on 21 April 1978 of a brain haemorrhage, following a fall down the stairs at a friend's house. It was one of those wasteful tragedies of unrealized potential. At the time of her death Sandy had spent three years out of the limelight, but had recently recorded her fourth solo album, *Rendezvous*, and only a few months previously had given birth to her first child, Georgia. At her funeral, they played Fairport's chilling 'Meet On The Ledge', and afterwards a solitary player piped the timeless lament, 'Flowers Of The Forest'.

*In 1974: Left to right (back row); Jerry Donahue, Trevor Lucas, (middle row); Dave Mattacks, Dave Pegg, Dave Swarbrick, (front); Sandy Denny.*

# Mama Cass Elliot

## 19 September 1941 - 29 July 1974

## by Ben Fong-Torres

*Cass Elliot was born in Baltimore on 19 September 1941. After early years spent on the New York folk scene she joined the Mamas and the Papas in 1965. At the Monterey Pop Festival in 1967, organized by John Phillips of the group, she dominated proceedings as a humorous master of ceremonies, and went on to become darling of the pop scene, playing host to numerous pop celebrities at her home in Laurel Canyon. In 1968 the group split up when Cass left to pursue other aspects of show business and had two solo hit records in that year. A regular chat show guest and part of the club/cabaret circuit, she appeared for two weeks at the London Palladium in 1974. On 29 July 1974 she was found dead in her London flat of a heart attack.*

The 'flower children' movement of the sixties may have taken root in San Francisco, but it took Los Angeles and New York to make it bloom commercially. Jefferson Airplane, Big Brother, and the Grateful Dead were free-form, bluesy and rowdy. It was left to the pros to put some gloss on the sounds of revolution, to romanticize it, to make it sell.

So we got Scott McKenzie with his 'San Francisco (Be Sure To Wear Flowers In Your Hair)'; the

Lovin' Spoonful; the Byrds; Harper's Bizarre. But most of all, we got the Mamas and the Papas, mixing east coast folk, west coast folk-rock, magnolia-sweet harmonies and coming up with a sound that the title of their first big hit described pretty well: 'California Dreamin'.

Like the golden era they serenaded, they didn't last long; it only took three years to move from first hit to last. But what an impact they made, with their emphasis on vocals, on rock solid back-up by

the cream of Hollywood's session musicians, with their organization of the first big rock festival ever: The Monterey International Pop Festival of 1967 (with Papa John Phillips and group manager Lou Adler at the forefront); and with their images. Especially those of the two women, the lovely, ethereal blonde, Michelle Phillips, and the fat, earthy angel, Cass Elliot.

If any voice, any figure, stood out among the Mamas and the Papas it was Mama Cass's. In her flowing tents of stage gowns, and with her humour making light of her weight (she was 5ft 5in and around 240 pounds) and numerous other subjects, she dominated their concert performances. At Monterey Pop, she told the audience that the Mamas and the Papas were the closing act at the festival because they were the tallest group, then wandered into this: 'Well, John's the tallest. And I'm the heaviest, except me and Pigpen [of the Grateful Dead] keep getting mistaken for each other. I tell 'em I'm the one with the tattoo...'

She was, in short, a natural master of ceremonies. She quickly

*Mama Cass's extrovert personality and sense of fun were as legendary as her size.*

*Mama Cass meets Jimi Hendrix at the 1967 Monterey International Pop Festival.*

became the queen of the L.A. pop scene. At home in Laurel Canyon, she played host to numerous musical and social jams; her visitors included Eric Clapton, Michael Bloomfield, and drummer Buddy Miles. Joni Mitchell wrote some of her first songs there, and three refugees from three groups got together in her living room and became Crosby, Stills and Nash.

Cass revelled in being a hippie, even if she was rich and famous (at least famous; when the group broke up, Cass was in debt for about six figures). She took acid and astrology seriously; after Chicago 1968, scene of the Democratic Convention riots, she became political. 'Maybe it's motherhood, too,' she said. 'I want to make a better world.'

Cass Elliot was born 19 September 1941, in Alexandria, Virginia. Her parents were opera fans and sang around the house. Cass herself did not begin singing until she was in college (the American University in Washington D.C.), where she joined a group with Tim Rose (co-author of 'Morning Dew') and James Hendricks. She and Hendricks later married and had a daughter, Owen.

In 1964, Cass was in New York with another folk group, the Mugwumps (John Sebastian, Sal Yanovsky and Denny Doherty). When Doherty hooked up with John and Michelle Phillips, Cass followed.

Years later, John would tell two widely varying stories about Cass's early connection with the group. One painted her as a groupie chasing after Doherty and trying, with little luck, to join the group. 'We wouldn't let her sing with us,' said Phillips. 'She'd rehearse with us, and then we'd say, "OK, Cass, serve some fucking drinks, we're going on stage." Finally we let her join the group.'

The other, much more affectionate story had the four taking acid the first night Cass met the Phillips. 'There was this fantastic rapport among the four of us, so we just sort of knew. We started singing, and it was obvious that it was just a matter of working it out.'

But the best early Mamas and Papas story of all has to do with the final touch added to Cass's voice. The Mamas and the Papas-to-be were in the Virgin Islands. As Cass told *Rolling Stone* interviewer Jerry Hopkins: 'They were tearing this club apart, putting in a dance floor. Some workmen dropped a metal plumbing pipe and it hit me on the head. I had a concussion and a bad headache for about two weeks and all of a sudden I was singing higher. My range was increased by three notes... honest to God!'

Thus equipped, the group moved to Los Angeles and had a string of hits: 'Monday Monday', 'California Dreamin', 'Dedicated To The One I Love', 'I Saw Her Again', 'Words Of Love', the autobiographical 'Creeque Alley', 'Twelve Thirty (Young Girls Are Coming To The Canyon)'. There were a few misses, primarily their live album from Monterey Pop and their difficult relationship with Dunhill Records, which resulted in a haphazard last album, an unsuccessful attempt at a reunion in 1971, and a seemingly endless stream of anthology albums.

It was Cass who broke up the group by leaving. She had a child, hated touring, and wanted to pursue the avenues of more conventional show business: nightclubs, television, film. After the break up in 1968, John and Michelle themselves dabbled in films; Denny Doherty pretty much disappeared. And it was Cass who managed to do well on her own, with two hits:

*The Mamas and the Papas: Dennis Doherty, Mama Cass, Michelle and John Phillips.*

'Dream A Little Dream Of Me' and 'Make Your Own Kind Of Music'. Her humour got her booked on a number of television shows, and, after a disastrous start in Las Vegas (due to bad nerves and tonsils) and an abortive hook-up with Dave Mason, she settled into the circuit of posh clubs and hotels.

And, in 1974, she was in one of the cities she loved most: London. Appearing at the Palladium – where she performed for two weeks – was an ambition come true. One night, as she left the hall, she saw the portrait of Judy Garland on display there. 'I know what it must have meant to that lady to be a hit here,' she told her manager, 'because I know what it means to me.'

Years before, she spoke about being drawn to England, 'especially to the Elizabethan period. I felt I was familiar with a lot of it, more than from what I read in school'. On the road with her group once,

she went to England. 'I drove to Stonehenge… I went to the Tower of London and it was familiar to me. I knew that I had been there. It was an irrefutable fact. It was like coming home for me.' She was talking about reincarnation.

And then, just two days after closing at the Palladium, in the early morning of 29 July, in the flat she was staying at – a flat belonging to the singer and composer Harry Nilsson – she died. It was cruelly ironic that the first reports had her choking after eating a sandwich in bed. That postmortem was corrected by a coroner; Cass died, at age 32, from a heart attack. But, he added, 'part of the heart muscle turned to fat due to obesity'.

Her last album was called *Don't Call Me Mama Any More*. But to the very end, Cass Elliot couldn't escape the image that gave her success in the first place.

*In 1968 Cass left the Mamas and the Papas to follow a solo career.*

# Marvin Gaye

## 2 April 1939 - 1 April 1984

### by Paolo Hewitt and Gavin Martin

*Marvin Gaye was born in Washington D.C. on 2 April 1939. As the son of a Pentecostal minister, he began his musical career playing the organ. After military service, Gaye sang with the Rainbows and then with the Marquees – later to become the Moonglows. In 1961 he teamed with the newly-formed Motown record label, first as a drummer, and then as a vocalist, where he recorded with a number of female artists, among them Tammi Terrell and Diana Ross. From 1963, every single he released went into the charts. Reaching the pinnacle of his career in 1969 with 'I Heard It Through The Grapevine', Gaye subsequently became disenchanted with Motown's overtly commercial outlook and by the beginning of 1983 he had severed all ties with them. After a dazzlingly successful solo album* Midnight Love *in 1983, Gaye moved back to live with his parents after a series of traumatic personal problems. He was shot by his father on 1 April 1984 after a heated argument.*

On a spring day in 1984, seventy-year-old Reverend Marvin Gaye Snr had an argument in his wife's bedroom with his son, also named Marvin. As a result, the Reverend shot him dead at point blank range. It was 1 April, the day before Marvin Jnr's forty-fifth birthday.

If you didn't know who Marvin Gaye was, you would probably think on reading that report that his father had simply lost his reason. And even if you did know, you might still come to the same conclusion – what possible justification could there be for his own father to shoot dead one of the finest soul singers to come out of the Motown stable? If music is to mean anything at all, then its richest quality must surely lie with its ability to communicate with true depth and honesty. In the work of Marvin Gaye, a

career lasting over 32 years, such an assessment is easily justified by most of the music he involved himself with.

As he worked through the smart pride and joy of early Motown, Gaye embraced a powerful emotional growth. He fused the elements and influences of those he worked with so that he could emerge in the second stage of his career with a depth and understanding for the sexual, social and spiritual. He met the supreme challenges that any musician or artist faces – how to combine personal experience with universal awareness, to celebrate his joys and sometimes quite chillingly lay bare his fears.

His work is in the truest sense of the word timeless; people will always be moved by the deeply sensuous 'Let's Get It On', just as there will always be someone somewhere haunted by his aching vocal on 'I Heard It Through The Grapevine'. And just as the all night sexual celebration of 'Midnight Love' will never lose its credence or vitality, so there will always be some kids practising their first dance steps to

*Marvin Gaye was presented as the stylish lover in the early days of Motown.*

'Hitch Hike' or 'Pride And Joy'. And as the world rushes headlong to its implosion so the frightening visions of *What's Goin' On* will become ever more relevant. In 30 years as a recording artist Marvin Gaye produced a body of work that few could hope to match or surpass. So what went wrong?

Marvin Pentz Gaye was born on 2 April 1939 in one of Washington D.C.'s poorer districts. His father was a minister and the young Marvin spent a lot of his childhood in church singing in his father's choir, which he later described as 'small but intense'. According to Marvin, his father was a strict disciplinarian with a no-nonsense approach towards religion. 'My father,' he told *New Musical Express* in 1982, 'was a Pentecostal and fire type. We're rootsy, our blackness and our spirituality is of a very real non-pretentious type. I rather like that.'

Gaye was educated at Randall Junior High School and Cardoza High School where, apart from displaying a keen interest in athletics, he spent a large portion of his time trying to shake off the stigma attached to him by his father's religious work. He saw it as 'quite a hardship on a child'. He constantly has to prove himself to his comrades that he's as normal as they are', he said. 'You have to do something rather bad or you're not accepted.'

At the age of 15, Gaye sang in his first group: a doo-wop outfit called the Rainbows. Other members included Don Covay and Billy Stewart. But under his father's orders, the singing soon stopped. Gaye joined the US Airforce where he spent a number of uneventful years, perhaps his most memorable experience being the loss of his virginity at the age of 16. 'It was with a hooker,' he revealed. 'I was in the Armed Forces and I'd just come off saltpetre, something they put in

*Marvin Gaye was one of the most innovative talents in black music.*

your food to keep your sexuality at a low ebb. They don't want any funny business in the barracks.'

After being discharged, Gaye returned home where he resumed his singing with the Rainbows, who later became the Marquees. He was spotted by Harvey Fuqua, a man who was subsequently to play a significant part in his career. Fuqua was a member of a famous fifties harmony outfit called the Moonglows, where he stayed until they disbanded. When that happened, both Gaye and Fuqua moved to Detroit to work on three new record labels: Harvey, Tri Phi and Anna. Fuqua had married Gwen Gordy, the sister of Berry Gordy, who had just acquired these labels, and put them under one banner: Motown.

Fuqua introduced Gaye to Gordy, and Gaye followed in Fuqua's footsteps by marrying another member of the Gordy family, Berry's sister Anna. It was to be the start of a long and turbulent relationship between Gaye and the Gordy family.

Gaye's first work at Motown was as a session drummer and he can be heard backing Smokey Robinson and the Miracles on their early singles. Marvin's first solo single was released in May of 1961. Entitled 'Let Your Conscience Be Your Guide', it was followed by his debut album *The Soulful Moods Of Marvin Gaye*. But it wasn't until a year later that he began to make his mark. Under producer William Stevenson, he cut 'Stubborn Kind Of Fellow' (where he was backed by the Vandellas on vocals), 'Hitch Hike' and 'Pride And Joy'. All these records bear a similar quality in their sparse instrumentation and solid backbeat which was to become the trademark of Motown. Indeed, Gaye's singles followed the development of Motown to a tee. As Holland, Dozier and Holland, amongst others, developed the famous Motown sound, so Gaye's records followed suit with increasing sophistication, leading up to his first major British success in 1969 with 'I Heard It Through The Grapevine'.

With Gordy concentrating the cream of Motown's songwriters

and producers on this young, good-looking vocalist, Gaye was quick to establish himself as *the* stylish lover. He was able, on a succession of records, to portray himself in a variety of guises: the hard-skinned stud on 'I'll Be Doggone', the pure romantic on 'How Sweet It Is'. 'I don't have a classic voice that comes from the diaphragm,' he once remarked, 'so I developed a style.'

Gaye was more than willing to go along with anything Motown desired of him. Check all the early press shots of Marvin and there he is, in smart but casual clothes, smiling as if he hadn't a care in the world. Motown was not about black consciousness or radicalism, it was about the sweet smell of success – exactly the image Marvin gave to the world.

To cement his lover persona, Gaye also recorded a succession of duets with female Motown singers. With Mary Wells there was the memorable 'What's The Matter With You Baby'. Then came Kim Weston and records such as 'What Good Am I Without You' and the often-covered 'It Takes Two'.

But the most successful and memorable association was the pairing of Marvin and Tammi Terrell. Once a member of the James Brown Revue, Terrell had joined Motown and released her own single, 'I Can't Believe You Love Me'. It was with Marvin that the pair of them shot to success. Presented as Motown's star-crossed lovers, they recorded three albums and eleven singles that all testified to the vocal chemistry between them. On songs such as 'Ain't Nothing Like The Real Thing', 'You're All I Need To Get By', 'If This World Were Mine', Gaye and Terrell successfully mapped out the blueprint for truly affecting duets; they also began to achieve recognition outside of America.

In 1969 Gaye released the haunting masterpiece, 'I Heard It Through The Grapevine', and his fame abroad quickly spread. 'Grapevine' was a Number 1 both in the States and the UK. With Terrell he had enjoyed nine Top 50 hits, and as the seventies dawned Marvin Gaye seemed to be in fine shape. But the twist of tragedy was just around the corner. On 16 March 1970 Tammi Terrell died in hospital following emergency operations for a brain tumour.

Gaye was devastated. Immediately he retreated from the studio and stage and went into self-imposed exile. When he finally emerged into the public spotlight he was completely unrecognizable from the Gaye that Motown had projected to the world. Gone was the sleek, smart singer of before, replaced by a heavier more philosophical man much troubled by the world he saw around him. With this 'new' Gaye came his personal statement of faith and values entitled *What's Goin' On*. By producing, arranging and largely self-writing this cataclysmic album, Gaye had flown in the face of the Motown production line simply by assuming all the responsibility himself.

The music he created bore scant relation to the familiar Motown sound but rather responded in a brilliant manner to the subjects – black consciousness, poverty, capitalism – that people like James Brown, the Staple Singers, Curtis Mayfield and Sly Stone had begun reflecting in their material. With *What's Goin' On* Gaye produced a timeless piece of work whose implications have never been fully realized by Gaye or others.

Motown's initial response to this masterpiece was one of typical reluctance. From Gordy downwards Motown just didn't want to know, souring their relationship with Marvin even further. After much resistance, they eventually put out *What's Goin' On* when Gaye told Gordy that it was fine by him if they didn't want to release it but never to expect any more work from him. Compromised completely, Gordy sanctioned its release. The album reached Number 6 in the US charts and made Motown over two million dollars. The three hit singles culled from it garnered over four million dollars between them.

Gaye's next venture was *Trouble Man*, a largely undistinguished film score, apart from the title track, that served as a filler between his next solo venture. That turned out to be *Let's Get It On*, an album which concentrated totally on the joys of love and sex and acted as a fine counterbalance to *What's Goin' On*'s desolate cry of despair. Assuming his previous persona as Love Man, but this time with a candour and depth not previously explored, Gaye was once again in full control of his talents, creating layer upon layer of lush, sensuous music tinged with the sound of heartbreak and set to the idea of sex as an all round liberating force. Once again he had created a body of work which still stands today as a contemporary collection of songs.

It would be three years until his next album finally appeared. In between, Gaye toured a little, cut an album with Diana Ross which, if not an artistic success, was at least a financial one, and indulged in his new found love of metaphysics, including his admiration for Carlos Castaneda. Gaye's awakening to this kind of knowledge was to be reflected in his music later on.

In 1976, Gaye reappeared with *I Want You*, which although not as coherent or as classy as his previous achievements, still contained proof of his unique talent in at least three of the songs. Gaye's explanation for this semi-disappointment was to lay the blame partially at Berry Gordy's doorstep. He told Cliff White: 'I don't *intend* to do anything...I wasn't gonna do it but

*When Gaye quit Motown in 1983 he was already suffering the effects of increasing drug abuse.*

Berry came and said, ''Listen man, dammit, you gotta do something, you been fooling round here for years.''...So he talked me into it right?...But I had no plans to produce anything on it myself because ninety per cent of the time, when I get mad I get very unproductive. And they keep me mad at them all the time by not treating me properly.' Motown remained tight-lipped on the subject, and after his British tour Gaye headed back to the studio to mix a live album and stunning single, 'Got To Give It Up', which proved beyond doubt his immense talent at creating trends – in this case subtle loose-limbed funk – rather than following them.

The variable quality of his output at this time may have been affected by his personal life. During 1976, Marvin's fourteen-year marriage to Anna Gordy came to an end and his latent instability spilled over into a suicide attempt in Hawaii. It is not insignificant that the method tried was to take at least 25 grams of cocaine in less than an hour. He himself recognized these bouts of instability when under personal pressure as a problem – he referred to them as his 'crazy periods'.

Once Gaye had divorced Anna and remarried his second wife, Jan, Anna sued Gaye and the High Court decided that she should receive the first $600,000 of the royalties from his next album. To fulfil this, Gaye produced *Here, Here My Dear*, a double album as tortured as it was cumbersome, which concerned itself totally with his relationship with Anna. Sometimes bitter and sometimes a celebration of love, it remains an odd album to get to grips with. Worse still, Gaye was charged with non-payment of taxes and served with a bankruptcy order. To meet his financial commitments, Gaye had to sell his studio to remain solvent.

To top it all, his wife Jan left him for one of his best friends, singer Teddy Pendergrass, who had benefitted enormously from filling the space Gaye had created. Crushed both financially and emotionally, Gaye moved to England and started work on his next album, *In Our Lifetime*, in a shattered depleted mood.

It was rumoured at the time that *Lifetime*, originally entitled *Love Man*, was intended to serve as Gaye's comeback, a conclusive proof of his master talent. When it did finally appear, it showed Gaye to be nowhere near that particular claim. Dour and uninspired in most parts, Gaye quickly disclaimed it, stating that Motown had relieved him of the master tapes and tampered irrevocably with them before he had had time to finish the album to his satisfaction.

By now, Gaye's use of drugs had become a well known fact and something he never categorically denied. His behaviour was erratic and unreliable – he failed to turn up in time for a charity concert attended by Princess Margaret on one occasion. Journalists turning up for interviews would often be met by a half-stoned man, rambling incoherently about his philosophies – which ironically contained anti-drug references – and his increasing bitterness with Gordy's Corporation.

Gaye saw himself as a pure artist and one who couldn't be expected to meet the commercial demands put upon him. So it was no surprise that in 1981 he would say, 'At this point I think I'd rather be with another record company. I've been told in no uncertain terms that if certain financial arrangements are made that I may leave the label, even though I am still technically under contract to them.'

At the start of 1983 Gaye completely severed his connection with Motown and signed with CBS. His exile in Europe continued and he headed for Belgium where under the supervision of Larkin Arnold and his long-time associate Harvey Fuqua, he completed the outstanding *Midnight Love*. If ever an artist vindicated the belief held in him, then Marvin Gaye did so triumphantly with this album. Confident, dynamic, fresh and invigorating, it was Gaye back on familiar territory, utilizing the synthesizer with a powerful approach. 'I have my own inimitable style,' he boasted at the time. 'And in that respect I try to do good music: music that has feeling, hope and meaning – all the things people are looking for.'

*Midnight Love* certainly fitted that description, as did its first single, 'Sexual Healing', a masterpiece of

sensitivity and innuendo which earned Marvin a Grammy award that year. The singles that followed all bore witness to Marvin Gaye's spectacular artistic rejuvenation and on the tide of his success he returned to America after a three year period of exile.

November of 1982 found him on as fine a form as any. He'd apparently overcome his problems, both personal and social, and was now able to bask in his glory. 'Certainly I've felt vindictive,' he said, 'and I still feel vindictively, and I certainly wish that those who have stepped on me will be punished. But a great measure of my satisfaction is that I have overcome many obstacles at this point and I have emerged rather victorious today. So I feel I have enough control to feel vindictive and turn the other cheek.'

Since his comeback, Gaye had been working with an official biographer on a forthcoming book and he also undertook his first American tour in years. But by all accounts the shows were not a success, either personally or financially. Gaye openly played up to his image by repeatedly blowing his nose audibly in front of the audience, a direct reference to the use of cocaine. However it didn't prevent Gaye from performing his unique version of the 'Star Spangled Banner' in a massive stadium at the opening of the baseball season.

It was in November 1983 that Marvin moved into the house in Los Angeles which he bought for his parents in the early seventies. Returning to the bosom of his family may have been a sort of cry for help, for it seems that in spite of outer confidence in his comeback, underneath Gaye was actually an emotional wreck. Misuse of drugs fuelled the paranoia which years of career and personal disappointments had engendered. Friends described how during his

last months he had threatened to take his own life, while at the same time being convinced that his life was in danger from unspecified outside forces. He took to carrying a gun, and sometimes remained in his bedroom at home for days on end, refusing food because he believed it to be poisoned. It was a vicious circle; money problems, creative uncertainties and failed marriages encouraged his drug use which in turn soured relationships with the friends and family members who had stayed loyal.

Gaye had always had problems relating to his father. As a youth he had worked hard, as he said, 'to lose the stigma of being a child of God'. It isn't hard to imagine the frustration and disappointment felt by his ageing fundamentalist father at the mess his son had made of his personal life, made more difficult to bear since the Minister faced it every day in his own home. It doesn't of course excuse his actions – shooting your own son dead over an argument about your wife, his mother, cannot be justified. But it has in its way a sort of logic, given the personalities involved, and as far as Marvin Gaye himself was concerned, appeared to represent a self-fulfilling prophecy.

The manner of Gaye's death gives a poignant resonance to his work. Marvin Gaye was not just a 'soul musician' but a musician who brought something unique to music, a gift that can never be surpassed. He was, for all his flaws, an *honest* individual who always remained as true to himself as he could, and if that caused friction, well, it goes with the territory. As he concluded, 'That's an artist. If he's good and if he's true to himself he can be just as wealthy as the other type of individual. But even if he never gets wealthy, he's wealthy anyway. He'll always be rich.'

Marvin Gaye was that man. For that alone, he should be celebrated.

# Lowell George

## 13 April 1945 - 29 June 1979

## by John Swenson

*Lowell George was born on 13 April 1945 in Hollywood. He learned guitar while at college and had formed his first band, Factory, and played with Frank Zappa, before creating Little Feat in 1970. Always a cult band, Little Feat's first two albums were not successful and new members were drafted in for the band's third album in 1973. After another split and reform the band recorded two more albums and successfully toured the UK in 1975. But George was now contributing little, drinking heavily and taking cocaine. After further touring and recording the group finally split up. While promoting his first solo album, George died of a heart attack on 29 June 1979.*

A dozen multicoloured spotlights flooded the stage and the band blasted back with a millionfold energy. '*Ro-o-o-o-o-o-o-oll*,' shouted Lowell George, his massive frame shaking from the effort, one hand throttling the microphone stand and the other clenched tightly to the neck of his guitar. '*Roll right through the night*,' came the echoing answer, not just from Paul Barrère and Bill Payne's backing vocals but from every throat in the hall as frenzied Little Feat fans stood on their seats and shouted their loyalty to America's most beloved band. A vertiginous set of sweet, swinging rock'n'roll was winding up with the anthem 'Feats Don't Fail Me Now', and George started to lead Barrère and Kenny Gradney in a surreal kick-dance of guitarists. The audience was going nuts, swept away by the giddy funk that Little Feat could squeeze out on a magical night.

That was the last I ever saw of Lowell George. Little Feat had just released its biggest album up to that point, *Time Loves A Hero*, and was touring the United States to pro-

mote it. The climax of the tour was a three-night stand at the Warner Theatre in Washington D.C., home of the band's most devoted audience.

At the time it was widely rumoured that George was dissatisfied with the band and would leave for a solo career. He had recently recovered from a bout of hepatitis and was working on a solo album; nobody, including the other members of the band, knew what to expect from him. Lowell was a subdued figure backstage; he performed brilliantly during the shows but disappeared afterwards. If he was harbouring a secret, nobody got it out of him.

George was virtually invisible on *Time Loves A Hero*, a fact that had been attributed to his illness, but the tension in the backstage atmosphere and the guarded way group members spoke about his role in Little Feat suggested a serious conflict. Keyboardist Bill Payne and guiatarist Paul Barrère had pretty well taken over the group, while George was estranged enough to travel separately from the rest of

*George was lead singer of Little Feat, which he formed in 1970 after leaving Mothers of Invention.*

the band, choosing to drive while the others flew.

'He told us each to take a bigger role in the group,' Payne explained at the time. 'But we had been starting to do that already. It really comes down to whoever has the hot hand with the songwriting – that's whose songs we end up recording. A lot of people seem to think George is holding out his songs for the solo album, but he's not even writing all the stuff on that record himself, he's doing a few covers, too.'

When I pressed Barrère about Little Feat's future without George, he said 'If George left, we wouldn't break up. We'd have to find another golden throat, but we could do it. But he's not gonna leave the band; no way that's gonna happen.'

Something was amiss, and George himself was not available for comment, but road manager Rick Harper gave a clue to George's status in the group. 'Lowell is an iconoclast,' said Harper. 'He doesn't have faith in anyone. But he does have faith in this group.'

In retrospect, what was happening in Washington makes sense. Lowell George was an unhappy man who saw his dreams of the perfect rock'n'roll band slipping away from him even though he approved of the group's musical maturation. The only place where he could resolve these differences was on stage, and it was there that he was transformed from the tired loner to the dynamic frontman of one of America's greatest groups.

Little Feat staggered through a couple more tours and two albums – the live *Waiting For Columbus* and Lowell's last studio production, *Down On The Farm* – before finally breaking up. George released his solo album, *Thanks I'll Eat It Here*, in 1979, just as the Little Feat breakup became public. During a tour to promote the record, George died of a heart attack on the morning before

he was to play a live broadcast in, of all places, Washington D.C.

A posthumous Little Feat album, *Hoy Hoy*, was a final tribute to George. 'The record wasn't supposed to be a Lowell George tribute,' explained Bill Payne, who supervised the collection. 'But with an overall view of the band, certainly, when we were looking at the material, I think a lot of it came from Lowell. That's one reason why Little Feat is not going to be a band without him. It's because he had so much to do with it.

'When Lowell died we finished the record as best we could; most of the tracks we still had to do over-dubs on, and there were some decisions to make. It was impossible to try and figure out what he wanted. Within the band itself emotions were running high and so it was very tough to finish the thing.'

Lowell George was born in 1945 in Hollywood. His father had moved there from Las Vegas in 1910 and became one of Tinseltown's top furriers. George was brought up in an environment cluttered with famous movie stars, some of whom, like Wallace Beery and W.C. Fields, were friends of his father's and some of whom, like Errol Flynn, were larger-than-life neighbours.

As a kid, George was something of an outcast. He was always overweight and was teased by the other kids as well as by his older brother, Willard. But music offered a useful retreat even in those early days. At the age of five Lowell picked up the harmonica and played a duet with his brother on 'The Ted Mack Amateur Hour'.

When he was 12 Lowell started studying classical flute and developed an interest in jazz. George went to Hollywood High School and studied as an art major at Valley Junior College, during which time he learned to play the guitar. When he became 21, he inherited some

money from his father and used it to bankroll a group called Factory, with childhood friend Martin Kibbee on bass and Warren Klein, alias Tornado Turner, sharing the guitar duties with George. The band's first drummer split suddenly to become a Moonie and George was forced to place an ad in the *Los Angeles Free Press* for a new drummer.

As luck would have it, one Richard Hayward chose this very time to pack in his gig pounding the skins for a local band in Ames, Iowa and make it out to L.A. for a shot at the big time. Hayward arrived at the Vine Street bus depot and spent his last quarter on a copy of the *L.A. Free Press*, hoping to find some work. Thus were assembled the first pieces of what eventually would become Little Feat.

Factory was managed by Herb Cohen, who was then also managing Frank Zappa. George met Zappa through the 'United Mutations' freakouts at which Factory opened for Zappa's band, Mothers of Invention. Zappa went on to produce some demos for Factory, but George split from Cohen's management and made a Factory LP for Uni that turned out to be a dismal flop. Factory split up; George went on to do sessions while the rest of the group stayed together under the name of the Fraternity of Man.

George went back to school, enrolling at L.A. City college as a music major, and studied with Ravi Shankar on the side. During this time, his trademark white funk guitar sound began to emerge. He was well suited to play the plunking, hard-edged guitar riffs that characterized songs like 'Dirty Water' by the Standells, one of the bands George sessioned with.

He also played with Zappa's group, which is where George really began to emerge. The only recorded legacy of this period is a single track on Zappa's *Weasles*

*Ripped My Flesh* compilation, 'Didja Get Any Onya', from 1969. George's distinctive vocal and slide guitar style on this track anticipated his later work with Little Feat.

Lowell's relationship with Zappa was tempestuous, but his stint with the Mothers provided the inspiration for Little Feat. Lowell contacted Hayward, who had been out of a gig since the Fraternity of Man packed it in, and the madcap drummer agreed to join the new band. Then bassist Roy Estrada quit Zappa to join the venture. All George needed was a keyboardist. Bill Payne had just quit his gig as musical director for the Viscounts show band in Santa Barbara and came to L.A. looking for a spot in Zappa's group. There was no opening in the Mothers, but Payne heard about George's project and decided to give it a try. The Little Feat chemistry was complete.

The first LP was split evenly between Payne's and George's material. There's a crude but moving version of 'Willin', George's truck-driving anthem, wistful tunes like the collaborative 'Strawberry Flats', strange flights of fancy like 'Hamburger Midnight', and a smattering of George's intense blues roots with Howling Wolf's '44 Blues'.

By the time of the second Little Feat album, *Sailin' Shoes*, the band's sound was pretty well defined and George had taken over most of the songwriting. This was the record that really started to establish Lowell George and Little Feat as an American institution.

The overall feeling of the record captures and freezes an attitude from the late sixties and early seventies, a tour de force of hard rocking blues that impressed the Rolling Stones strongly enough to prompt them to ask if they could join Little Feat for a jam at one of their gigs (a request, incidentally, that was refused). George wrote some of his best material for this album, including the title track and 'Easy To Slip'.

*Sailin' Shoes* also showed George off as one of rock's finest singers. He breaks up the metre of the lyrics on 'Cold Cold Cold' and 'Apolitical Blues' like a master blues vocalist, repeating phrases and pausing in rhythmic counterpoint to the instrumental track. He re-does 'Willin' as a stone country ballad and addresses 'Texas Rose Cafe' in the same manner, then pulls out all the stops for his frenzied, high-energy delivery on 'Teenage Nervous Breakdown' and 'Tripe Face Boogie'. The latter tune, written by Payne and Hayward, is a medium for the band's flashy instrumental chops and George's trademark, up-the-fretboard slide guitar playing.

The first of Little Feat's celebrated break ups occurred after the dismal reaction to *Sailin' Shoes*, which sold very few records and left the band destitute. Estrada quit to join Captain Beefheart, and George decided to augment the line-up. Bassist Kenny Gradney, fresh from Delaney and Bonnie's touring group, joined up and brought percussionist Sam Clayton along. A second guitarist, Paul Barrère, was added to free George for more slide and vocal work.

This new, inter-racial Little Feat was even better than George had hoped. They came storming back from the edge with an album, *Dixie Chicken*, that solidified their fanatical following around the country.

*Dixie Chicken* is an almost perfect album in the delicacy of its pacing and the rich, exciting mix of material.

Though, musically, *Dixie Chicken* signalled the beginning of the golden age of Little Feat, commercially it was a failure and once again the band stared into the abyss. George scrambled around desperately to get enough session work to keep the group going through these lean times, a move that resulted in classic match-ups pairing Little Feat with jazz drummer Chico Hamilton and white R&B vocalist Robert Palmer.

What made Little Feat great was that it was truly a band. It wasn't just George's singing or writing or playing or creative direction that made it work; it was the whole package: that seductively undulating rhythm section, the little fills and details that set Little Feat apart. Sure there was tension, but it was the tension that comes from truly creative people working hard toward an ideal. The rest of the band would sound hollow without George. And Lowell George could never have assembled a group better than Little Feat. That's why George, in spite of his incredible talent and the opportunities he was given to play with virtually anyone he wanted, tried to keep the band going right up to his last breath. Because Little Feat was still great even as it was disintegrating. In spite of how painful it was for Payne to complete *Down On The Farm*, the band still sounded terrific on the record. You know that somehow, had Lowell George lived, Little Feat would have played again. That's one of the excruciatingly painful things about his death.

'It's so tragic, such a waste,' Payne lamented. 'Lowell was a genius. He could do so many things and he just burned himself away. We've seen it happen to some of our most gifted musicians, and it's a tremendous loss to the world. Who knows what Jimi Hendrix or Lowell George could have done had they lived? They might have been able to bring about whole new approaches to music. Who can say that Lowell might not have been a Beethoven or Bach had he lived? I can hardly bear to think about it.'

# Jimi Hendrix

## 27 November 1942 - 18 September 1970

## by Charles Shaar Murray

*Jimi Hendrix was born in Seattle, Washington on 27 November 1942. After a brief spell in the US paratroopers (1961-3), Hendrix started to earn a living as a musician. Spotted by Chas Chandler of the Animals, he was taken to London in 1966 and joined Noel Redding and Mitch Mitchell to form the Jimi Hendrix Experience. With two hit singles in 1967, the impact of the radical Hendrix sound and image was extreme. Invited to appear at the 1967 Monterey Pop Festival, his performance became legendary. After 1968 – Hendrix's most successful year – his luck changed. Internal conflicts led to the ultimate collapse of the Experience and he was involved in legal and business difficulties. After busting him for heroin in Toronto in 1969, the police continued to harass him about his drug habit. After playing two more sets (Woodstock 1969, Isle of Wight 1970), Hendrix died in London on 18 September 1970 after inhaling vomit following barbiturate intoxication.*

Strictly speaking, Jimi Hendrix's career as an active participant in world pop music lasted four years. In that time, he became one of the most influential and imitated electric guitarists of all time, a man whose work audibly demolished barriers between Delta

blues, soul funk, free jazz and hard rock. He created sounds with a Fender guitar, a couple of effects pedals and a wall of amplification which would remain inaccessible to others until the advent of mass-production synthesizer technology. The rock'n'roll industry of the late sixties turned him into a cultural icon of massive proportions, and with his music if not with his public statements provided a perfect and awesome account of the American nightmare.

He wanted but never succeeded in writing a 'new anthem' for America, but he shut down the sixties by rewriting the old one. After three days of love, peace and self-delusion by four hundred thousand mainly white youths in a huge field near Woodstock in upstate New York, Jimi Hendrix – in the most committed and responsible manner possible, with the utmost dignity and with loving fervour – performed the musical equivalent of burning his nation's flag. 'The Star Spangled Banner' was slashed to ribbons, charred almost – but not quite – beyond recognition, clear trumpet-like notes of trembling purity gleaming fitfully through the smoke from torch-lit buildings, illuminated by the blue pulse of police lights. Whole galaxies of American music collided in Hendrix's hands on that spectral, chilly morning: the eerie whine of Robert Johnson's slide guitar, the transcendent glossolalia of Coltrane's horn squeezed through the harsh, metallic tonalities of rock. Hendrix did more than simply describe or discuss America: he created it right there on the spot. The battle for the nation's soul was symbolically enacted,

*Jimi Hendrix epitomized sixties' flamboyance.*

*The Jimi Hendrix Experience. Left to right: Mitch Mitchell, Noel Redding and Jimi Hendrix.*

the shining theme dissolving into explosions, sirens, gunfire and the unmistakeable sound of a soul in the throes of mortal agony, and finally re-emerging injured beyond all recovery or repair. An old and familiar tune played by a black man on a white guitar back when it was already too late.

Hendrix was a quintessential American artist, born on 27 November 1942 in Seattle, Washington. He died in London on 18 September 1970, barely four years after arriving in that city to make his fortune. After a long spell as a freelance soul guitarist travelling around the States backing the likes of Little Richard, the Isley Brothers and King

Curtis, Hendrix was spotted playing in a New York club and brought over to England by Chas Chandler, a musician turned impresario who had started out as the bassist for the original Animals. Chandler surmised – quite correctly – that England, which was then crowded with young guitarists eagerly exploring the then-unmapped territories of extended blues-rock soloing and massive amplification, would be far readier for Hendrix than the US soul circuit, which loved Hendrix's extensive repertoire of funk rhythms but considered his extravagant soloing somewhat out of order. Hendrix could beat any British guitar hot shot at his own particular caper: his dexterity and audacity far surpassed Jeff Beck, his blues playing had a fluidity and passion which Eric Clapton could not

match, and his violent, mesmeric stage act went far beyond even Pete Townshend's. Plus he was black, and unlike the soul and ska fans, British blues audiences had no contemporary black figurehead.

Hendrix's friend the late white bluesman Michael Bloomfield, once wrote, 'In his playing I can really hear Curtis Mayfield, Wes Montgomery, Albert King, B.B. King and Muddy Waters. Jimi was the blackest guitarist I ever heard. His music was deeply rooted in pre-blues, the oldest musical forms, like field hollers and gospel melodies. From what I can garner, there was no form of black music that he hadn't listened to and studied.' Nevertheless, he made his reputation with white sidemen, white management and a white audience, and his music was re-exported to the States as the last word in British hard rock. To this day it is Heavy Metal fans who are most eager to claim him as one of their own, and every ranking Heavy Metal guitar player will pay verbal and musical tribute to him, although their absorption of his music generally stops short at ham-fisted mimicry of his best-known stunts. Hendrix's musical vocabulary was developed over a long period of time for a specific set of purposes, to express what could not be expressed through conventional means. The surface flash was attractive and attention-grabbing, but it was never intended to be the whole show. In his lowest moments, Hendrix feared that that was all that was wanted from him.

Duke Ellington's instrument – or so the one-liner says – was his orchestra. Jimi Hendrix transformed his instrument into an orchestra. He loved the straight-ahead rock and roll bamalama rhythms and the snakier shift and bounce of soul, and he got to where he could make a little riff rebound and dance like a pinball machine:

*Jimi's performance at the 1967 Monterey Pop Festival was legendary and made him a star in the USA.*

catch it on the way down, hit the flipper and send it all the way back up again. He loved the shimmering, floating drone of the slide guitars of the Delta, the way Muddy Waters took the thin, piercing acoustic bottleneck sound of the haunted poet Robert Johnson and blew it up until it was a sound as big as a house and as sharp as a knife, filled it full of electricity until it loomed over you like King Kong, inexpressibly huge and yet able to hover and dart and hum. He loved the blazing tenor saxophones of rock'n'roll and jump blues, that *vocal* quality, the way a note lasted as long as the player's lungs held

out or rasped and squealed just like a voice could, the explosive punctuation that a good horn section could bring to a tune.

He had heard the exquisite float and sting of B.B. King's guitar, and the wilder and more radical blues guitar sounds of Ike Turner, Buddy Guy and Johnny Guitar Watson, and he knew from both his own experience and from some of the experimental records by the avant-garde British rock bands that when you over-amplified a guitar, weird things happened to the sound: it got more like a voice, more like a horn. And the more you jacked the signal up the more it transformed. Plus there was one thing more, as his biographer David Henderson has suggested, in his superb *'Scuse Me While I Kiss The Sky:* as an army para-

chutist (before he was put out of action with an ankle injury) Hendrix heard the sounds of jet engines and the rush of air around him as he jumped, the sound of the heavens, the sound of beyond. He heard all of this, and he wanted all of it. He discovered his mission, which was to wring all of this from a guitar, a Fender orchestra that hung around his neck. At this time, the height of guitar technology was the fuzz box and reverb. Can you imagine how nuts everybody must have thought Jimi Hendrix was? Crazy man wants to sound like a horn or a jet plane...

As a backing musician for Little Richard and King Curtis and the Isley Brothers, Jimi Hendrix had a chance to use his encyclopaedic knowledge of soul riffs to refine his astonishingly fluid sound and technique, but there was no way that his manic orchestral funk experiments would fit into any-body else's format. Soul music is an intensely disciplined form, and it always has been: from Ray Charles to James Brown to Sly Stone to Earth Wind And Fire, soul has always meant a total commitment to the leader's vision and a total precision in the execution of that task. No great soul record has ever been made without that discipline, and even though Hendrix was per-fectly capable of doing just about anything that any leader on a soul or R&B session would demand, his vision was ultimately so different from anybody else's that it was inevitable that he would have to lead his own band. So he relocated from Harlem to the Village, led his own scratch band, sat in for a few weeks with white bluesman John Hammond Jr (the son of the John Hammond who mattered) and got discovered and whisked off to England by Chandler.

To this day, Hendrix is inextri-cably linked with the format that later became known as the 'power

*Jimi Hendrix's musical brilliance and outrageous personality made him one of the mythical figures of the sixties.*

trio'. Whether augmented by a vocalist or not, the 'power trio' is the basic unit of guitar, bass and drums unencumbered by any additional instrumentation. Though Hendrix himself had initial doubts about his own qualities as a vocalist, Bob Dylan had demonstrated more than effectively that if a singer had a distinct personal identity and an ability to communicate, a conventional 'good voice' was superfluous. All that was required – since truth automatically implied beauty – was a solid rhythm section and a good tune, and Jimi Hendrix would do the rest himself.

Both Chandler and Hendrix were agreed that Billy Roberts' tune 'Hey Joe' (previously recorded by the Byrds on their *5th Dimension* album and by folk-rocker Tim Rose) was the right tune in question, so that was that. The musicians eventually selected by Hendrix and Chandler for the rhythm section of what was to become the Jimi Hendrix Experience were of widely differing musical environments, but their collective approach was perfectly suited for Hendrix's all-out assault on the jaded sensibilities of the London club scene. Drummer Mitch Mitchell had played with Georgie Fame's Blue Flames, a popular club band whose music effortlessly fused soul, blue-beat, swing and calypso, which gave Mitchell a far greater rhythmic sophistication than the average rock-band thrasher, while bassist Noel Redding was an unemployed rock guitarist willing to play bass if the job looked good. Like many British musicians of that period, they had a tremendous respect verging on awe for black

Americans in the abstract, but quite a few problems dealing with a genuine black American contemporary, which meant that the fact of Hendrix's colour radically affected the manner in which he was presented and perceived.

His presence on the London rock scene lent it authenticity and endorsement, simply because of the fluid mastery with which he handled the soul, blues and rock materials which were so demonstrably his birthright. In the States, Hendrix was simply another scuffling session guitarist with a taste for weird noises, but to the London scene as it was in 1966, he was Black Music Incarnate, conferring a seal of approval on the new rock. He came to them via Chas Chandler, he played with two of their own and he wore their fashions, customizing them as he went. Within weeks, half the ace faces in London had permed their hair to match Hendrix's. And at the same time, the whole issue of racism in the music business was conveniently ignored. Redding recalls the days of 'me and this coon from America. Yes, that's what I used to call him. Jimi loved that – he really dug it'. One wonders just how much Hendrix was prepared to put up with in order to stay cool with the Englishmen who were finally – *finally* – going to make him a star, get his music heard. One of his road managers, Gerry Stickells, summed up the situation with blinding clarity: 'To me Jimi wasn't a black man – he was a white man. He didn't think like a coloured guy, and he certainly didn't appeal to a coloured audience at all. He wasn't playing coloured music. Not that he wasn't sympathetic to their cause, he just didn't really think about it. You could make jokes with him about it.' In other words, Hendrix's blackness

*Hendrix's violent and mesmeric stage act often culminated in the burning of his guitar.*

*Hendrix on stage at Woodstock in 1969.*

was only acknowledged insofar as it was an aspect of style, as part of his stock-in-trade, his appeal, his credentials. It is not surprising that white audiences responded to him instantly, while blacks treated him with suspicion for several years. It was a white critic, Robert Christgau, who reacted to Hendrix's US premier at the 1967 Monterey Festival by denoucing him as 'a psychedelic Uncle Tom', but he undoubtedly represented the views of many black listeners as well.

By the time of that Monterey appearance, Hendrix had clinched three British top ten singles ('Hey Joe', 'Purple Haze' and 'The Wind Cries Mary') and a best-selling debut album, *Are You Experienced.*

He had been booked for the Festival on the personal recommendation of Paul McCartney, and Brian Jones had flown over specifically to introduce him. His devastating showmanship, his left-handed assault on his guitar, his armoury of sonic and visual tricks – playing the guitar T-Bone Walker or Buddy Guy style behind his head, between his legs or with his teeth – and his shy, friendly cool enabled him to follow the Who onstage and beat them at their own game. Like Joplin and Otis Redding, Hendrix established himself with 'the love crowd' that night, and like Redding, Hendrix presented a non-threatening black image to the white audience. He wore *their* clothes, took *their* drugs, wanted to be with them. He didn't hate them!

Many people remember Hendrix

as a man who had great difficulty saying 'no' to anyone. They also remember him as a man subject to occasional fits of almost terrifying rage. Pete Townshend recalls Hendrix calling him a 'fucking honky' on the night of Monterey, which probably demonstrates the extent to which Hendrix trusted Townshend and felt open around him. Undoubtedly he did feel the constraints of the white rock and roll straitjacket he was in. When he disbanded the Experience in late 1969 to work with black musicians – drummer Buddy Miles and his old army buddy Billy Cox on bass – his management's reaction was extremely negative. Chandler had quit and left Hendrix's affairs in the hands of his partner Mike Jeffery, and Jeffery objected strongly to the replacement of photogenic hippies like Redding and Mitchell, and to the funkier, less poppy material which Hendrix was beginning to perform. Eventually, Miles and Hendrix fell out, but Cox stayed until the end. Owing to various financial calamities and the odd bit of mindfucking by the front office, Hendrix found himself a virtual slave. His record royalties placed in escrow over a court case, he was forced to stay out on the road pumping out the old hits to an audience that wanted an animated poster of its favourite fantasies just in order to keep afloat and to keep paying the bills on Electric Lady, the dream studio that he was building down on 8th street in New York. Just at the time when he felt the most urgent need to take his music somewhere else, he was forced to keep pleasing a management that simply wanted to make as much money from him as possible – short term, quick killing – and an audience that wanted him to stay just where he was.

Gradually, black and white audiences alike had began to suss Hendrix as more than the 'electric nigger dandy' (to quote one of those US rock critics who think they're hip enough to call black people niggers) and Heavy Metal King that his original act implied. As early as 1967 he had jammed with Rahsaan Roland Kirk, the brilliant blind multi-instrumentalist whose unique breathing techniques allowed him to hold notes indefinitely on flute, saxophone or any number of other instruments, and to play one or more horns simultaneously, and Kirk had given him the kind of recognition that would not normally be given to a rock guitarist. Miles Davis had listened long and hard to the work of Hendrix and his fellow soul rebel Sly Stone, and with *Bitches' Brew* had virtually redefined jazz to accommodate these influences. Even today, Miles' guitarist Mike Stern admits, 'At Avery Fisher Hall

last year he went over and turned my amp up at one point, and he's always saying things to me like, ''Play some Hendrix! Turn it up or turn it off!'' Miles loves Hendrix.' At after-hours jams, he played with John McLaughlin, Tony Williams, Larry Coryell and Larry Young, and – a week before his death – had opened discussions with Gil Evans, the brilliant arranger who had worked with Davis on such epochal recordings as *Sketches Of Spain* and *Porgy And Bess* about a Carnegie Hall concert in which Evans' band would play arrangements of Hendrix's music with Hendrix himself as the featured soloist. The project was eventually resumed in 1974, and *The Gil Evans Orchestra Plays The Music Of Jimi Hendrix*, though sorely lacking in the touches that Hendrix himself would have brought to it, reveals one thing with breathtaking clarity: the orchestral nature of Hendrix's art. All the orchestrations are derived from Hendrix's own parts, and were virtually complete when he had finished recording them.

Jimi Hendrix died from an accidental overdose of barbiturates, leaving behind a vault full of tapes in varying stages of completion. A double album called *First Rays Of The New Rising Sun* was almost ready, and was eventually released as two separate records *Rainbow Bridge* and *Cry Of Love*. His music has been mixed and remixed by a variety of engineers and producers, it has had original rhythm section tracks erased and replaced by session musicians, it has been endlessly repackaged. Just about every note that Hendrix ever recorded has been exhumed and released in some form or another. And what is plain from all of it is that the man had hardly begun. In those four years, Hendrix placed himself at the crossroads of modern pop, pulping the barriers between rock, soul, jazz and blues. Like a finely-ground lens

he gathered up disparate beams of light and integrated them – or, to be more precise, *re*-integrated them. His devices and innovations are now part of a common musical language, open and available to all. Who else has influenced artists as superficially irreconcilable as Bob Marley, Miles Davis, Eddy Grant and Eddie Van Halen?

The question inevitably arises: what would Hendrix have played if he had lived? His last musical vision had been of a 'Handel-Bach-Muddy Waters-flamenco thing' of a big band that would play arranged music, a far cry from the occasionally augmented rock trio which had been his previous format. Certainly he could have played just about anything: the ease with which his techniques have branched into soul via guitarists like Ernie Isley, or the harmolodic jazz-funk of James Blood Ulmer, or even into King Sunny Ade's juju and the Wailers' reggae demonstrates the universality of his music. Even the instrument he played, the Fender Stratocaster, had been associated principally by Americans with Buddy Holly and the surfing bands and by Brits with Hank Marvin and the Shadows before he made its possibilities clear, revealing aspects of the instrument that shocked the manufacturers.

But finally, what places Jimi Hendrix in the pantheon of crucial black American artists is the quality of his expression and the utter authenticity of the emotion he conveys. Hendrix's work is not about sex and drugs and guitars: it is about the human soul. Like Armstrong, like Robert Johnson, like Charlie Parker and Billie Holliday and John Coltrane, Jimi Hendrix took his listeners far beyond instruments or personalities or situations. To listen to Jimi Hendrix is to *transcend* Jimi Hendrix. His music never manipulates, it *moves*.

# Buddy Holly

## 7 September 1936 - 3 February 1959

## by John Tobler

*Buddy Holly was born Charles Hardin Holley on 7 September 1936 in Lubbock, Texas. He started playing the guitar in 1948. Success performing with a school friend led to a regular radio appearance and in 1956 Buddy obtained a record contract with Decca. By 1957, under producer Norman Petty, Holly formed the Crickets. With Buddy singing lead and solo, they released a string of hits throughout 1957 and '58. Buddy's marriage in 1958 to Puerto Rican, Maria Elena Santiago, caused family tensions and led to a rift with Petty and the Crickets. In early 1959, Buddy joined the touring Winter Dance Party and while travelling to a show in Minnesota was killed in a plane crash on 3 February 1959.*

When Don McLean released his hit song 'American Pie' in 1972, you knew at once what he was talking about. 'The day the music died' was for him 3 February 1959, when a charter plane travelling from Mason City, Iowa, and heading for Fargo, North Dakota, took off in a slight snowstorm, and crashed on farmland only ten miles away. Its four occupants were killed: the pilot, and his three celebrity passengers, J. P. Richardson ('the Big Bopper'), Ritchie Valens – and Buddy Holly.

Thirty years on, the generation that was in its teens in the late fifties is still in mourning – frozen in a time-warp by Holly's songs. He was only 22 when he died, recently married, and in three years as a recording artist had written and recorded a legacy of songs which has steadily grown in stature since his death, making him one of the genuine legends of popular music. As Philip Norman wrote recently, 'Holly was where nearly everything began.'

Buddy Holly was born Charles Hardin Holley on 7 September 1936

in Lubbock, Texas. His musical talent was apparent by the age of 15, and in keeping with his Texan background his early efforts were mainly country and hillbilly-orientated. His career began with a familiar pattern of unsuccessful recordings in various styles, but it was his association with Norman Petty at Petty's studio in Clovis, New Mexico that helped achieve the break-through. Teamed with Jerry Allison and Joe B. Mauldin as the Crickets, Holly's first hit came in 1957 with 'That'll Be The Day', one of the true classics of rock'n'roll.

Buddy Holly never looked back. His music was the ultimate 'cross-over' (he and the Crickets were once booked on a tour with all-black musicians because the promoters hadn't realized they were white), and it incorporated a number of important innovations, which had enormous impact on the emerging rock scene in Britain in the early sixties. The Crickets consisted of the classic line-up of guitars, bass and drums with a lead singer. Holly's espousal of the Fender Stratocaster ensured its position as the leading brand of electric guitar for more

*Holly left a legacy of songs which make him one of the genuine legends of popular music.*

*The Crickets. Left to right: Jerry Allison, Joe B. Mauldin and Buddy Holly.*

than two decades. He was also one of the first singer-songwriters – a young man writing convincingly about young people's preoccupations. And he didn't mind wearing glasses.

Holly's career was tantalizingly brief. Speculation about what might have happened is fruitless, but it is significant in assessing his lasting contribution to rock, that he had not had time to make an inferior record. His posthumous releases point clearly to the way he was going – up. It is no coincidence that when Paul McCartney was urged to purchase a songwriting catalogue for investment purposes, he chose the Buddy Holly catalogue. Although this catalogue numbers less than 100 titles, there seems to be a never-ending queue of singers and groups waiting to pay tribute to his skill by covering Holly songs, a substantial

number of which have been hits. Cliff Richard had an early eighties hit with 'True Love Ways'; The Beatles covered 'Words of Love' on their *Beatles for Sale* album; John Lennon cut 'Peggy Sue' for his mid-seventies *Rock'n'Roll* LP; The Rolling Stones' first British Top 3 hit was a Crickets B-side, 'Not Fade Away'. Among other notable Buddy Holly cover versions are several by Linda Ronstadt, including 'It's So Easy', 'That'll Be The Day' and 'It Doesn't Matter Any More', all of which became American Top 50 hits during the 1970s; 'Well...All Right', which was recorded by Santana and Blind Faith; 'I'm Gonna Love You Too', by Blondie; 'Raining In My Heart', by Leo Sayer; and 'Oh Boy!' by British rock revivalists Mud, whose *a cappella* version of the song topped the British charts in 1975.

Buddy Holly's death gave rise to the inevitable exploitation of unreleased recordings and demos to

which all the musicians in this book have to some extent been subjected. However most of Holly's material enhances the singer's reputation rather than the other way round. Many of the unreleased tracks became hits in their own right, especially in Britain, and there can be no doubt about the validity of their release. Many of them, such as 'Brown Eyed Handsome Man', 'Reminiscin'' and 'Bo Diddley', retain their freshness today. These tracks were given new instrumental backings by a group managed by Norman Petty and, although not every track 'improved' in this way was successful, it is clear that during the years immediately following Buddy's death, it was Norman Petty who was the key figure in keeping the singer's name alive and his sound authentic in the minds of the public.

Norman Petty and Buddy Holly were in dispute at the time of Buddy's death, and Petty is often cast in the role of evil manager, beggaring the singer by withholding his royalties and thereby forcing Holly onto the fateful Winter Party tour during which the accident occurred. But like most such stories, it is never as simple as that. Buddy had split with Petty and the Crickets earlier in the year in part because he wanted to remain on the East Coast with his new wife, Maria Elena, and he was keen to pursue a career in New York City, the heart of the music business. Petty, naturally, was less keen to see his most successful protégé move out of his control, and he was not the first – nor would he be the last – manager to use the mechanism of royalty retention while a legal battle was fought. Holly was short of money – and his latest solo release, 'Heartbeat', was not going anywhere, so the tour provided income and a chance to promote it. Had Norman Petty been able to foresee the results of his machinations it is obvious he would never have followed the course he did.

Despite the continual plundering of his small recorded legacy – released as much to satisfy the public's need as for reasons of exploitation – Buddy Holly remains an heroic figure, not only among those who remember his excellent music at first hand, but also to newer fans who have been introduced to it via the many other artists who have recorded his songs, and, incidentally, through the constant stream of radio and TV tributes that have been broadcast every ten years since his death. Although his life was sadly abbreviated, it ironically prevented him from diluting his achievements, something which few of his contemporaries have avoided, and thereby ensured him a pioneering position in the progress of rock'n'roll over the past thirty years.

*Holly was the first singer-songwriter to write convincingly about young people's problems.*

# Brian Jones

## 28 February 1942 - 3 July 1969

## by Nick Kent

*Brian Jones was born on 28 February 1942 in Cheltenham to middle-class parents. After dropping out of public school, he taught himself a variety of instruments. He gigged with local jazz bands before meeting Mick Jagger and Keith Richard in London in the early sixties. Together they formed the Rolling Stones in 1963. The group was famous within the year and rich by 1964. By 1967, Jones was suffering from the strain of touring, adverse publicity and multiple drug convictions and, losing the limelight to Jagger, and his girlfriend to Richard, he became increasingly paranoid. Dropped by the Rolling Stones in June 1969, he drowned in the swimming pool at his home on the night of 2–3 July.*

To any of the countless prolific dreamers of my generation – those of us who were adolescents in the sixties – Brian Jones meant something and from the moment we made contact with his perfect blond impudence, it was weird love at first sight. When I first saw him live with the Rolling Stones it was early 1964, I was twelve, they were only weeks away from being the biggest thing to hit England since the bubonic plague – and oh, I will never forget it. They looked simply out of this world, like a new delinquent

aristocracy and they played music of a stunning arrogance and unbridled potency. And they had Brian Jones who really appeared like their leader that night; with his china-cat smile of evil assurance. He looked to me like a young man who had everything – charm, beauty, grace, success, infamy - every wondrous virtue this world could hope to offer and for a long time afterwards his vision epitomized everything I in turn could hope to aspire to.

The next time I saw the Rolling Stones live five years later, Brian

Jones was there but not in the flesh. He was just a huge cardboard cut-out representation at the side of the stage. He was five days dead and the Rolling Stones, cool and disengaged as ever, were playing at his wake. The strange thing was how little genuine sorrow there was emanating from the 250,000 – plus crowd gathered at Hyde Park. A sense of loss, perhaps, but not sorrow. In a *Rolling Stone* obituary already circulating that afternoon, Greil Marcus stated that when he heard that Jones was dead he felt no sense of shock, only that this was the most natural thing to happen to this tormented narcissus. It was true: the way Brian Jones lived his life he had nowhere to fall but into the grave.

He was born on 28 February 1942 in Cheltenham and it was genteel, conservative Cheltenham as much as drugs, stardom or notoriety which was to prove his undoing. Certainly Keith Richard has strong views on this. 'Brian was from Cheltenham, a very genteel town full of old ladies. It's a Regency thing, you know, Beau Brummel and all that. Just a seedy place full

*Brian Jones dazzled the rock world flaunting sexual freedom with his flamboyant style.*

of aspirations to be an aristocratic town. It rubs off on anyone who comes from there...He (Brian) had to conquer London first, that was his big thing. He felt happy when we'd made it in London, when we were the hip band in London. For me and Mick, it didn't mean a thing, because it was just our town.'

His mother was a rather prim, religiously finicky woman. His father, a small Welshman from whom his son gained some of his singular looks, was quiet and deferential, but inwardly seething with terrible anger. He had an elder sister, Jacqueline, who would be identified as a source of intense childhood jealousy on Jones' side by a psychiatric report, one of many in his last years alive. 'He never felt loved', concluded the report.

He was obviously a prolific dreamer, and a prolific hustler too. From a very early age Brian Jones must have learnt just how contagiously precociously charming he could be and how by using this easy charm he could go a long way to getting whatever he wanted. Apparently excellent scholastically, he nonetheless bucked that system by staging a mini-revolt at school and getting turfed out as a result. If there was ever a turning point in his life, it was probably here but it's hard to tell. After all he was always a pretty audacious guy: already a girl was pregnant, the family shamed and he didn't really seem to care. He let that easy charm grease his path away from the spectre of provincial ruination time and time again. Meanwhile he was being audaciously awful as a saxophone player in a Duane Eddy-styled combo, the Ramrods, but as a guitarist and harmonica player he started showing weird promise. He became a rhythm'n'blues obsessive, and, as his best instrumental contributions to Rolling Stones records will later readily attest, this was the music that he had

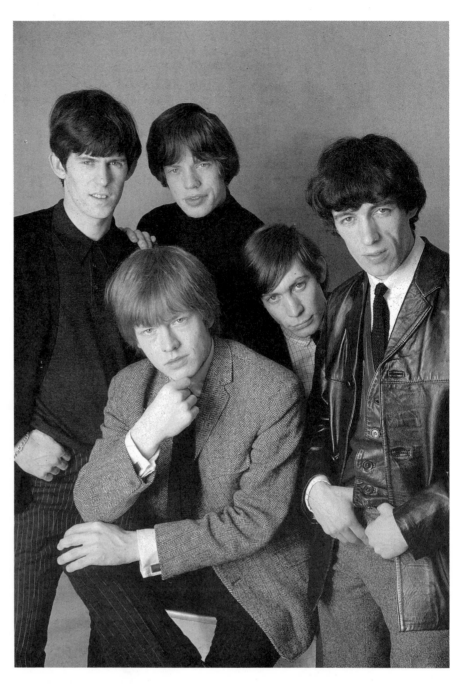

The Rolling Stones. Left to right:
Keith Richard, Brian Jones, Mick Jagger,
Charlie Watts and Bill Wyman.

the greatest feel for: he aped old blues stylists like Jimmy Reed and Elmore James and planned on changing his name to Elmo Lewis, moving to London and becoming a big wheel. In 1961 in a tiny Cheltenham club, Alexis Korner, performing with Chris Barber's Jazz Band, was accosted by an extremely intense young man who was also extremely inebriated. 'It was Brian, of course. He was accompanied by a mate of his, I seem to recall, who said nothing. Not that anyone else could, because Brian was this pent-up ball of obsessive energy, talking away ten-to-the-dozen in an incredibly intense manner.'

That's how people talk when they reminisce about Brian Jones.

'I vividly recall the first time I met Brian but I can't for the life of me remember where I first met Mick,' Korner once told me and he was being honest not bitchy because already Brian Jones had reinvented himself, he was larger than life and on fire for acclaim. And of course he was always hustling, stealing and petty pilfering. More often than not he appears to have got caught, yet each time he slipped through with only a caution. This also happened in London just after he'd moved down: he was sacked from a record shop for having his hand in the till.

But by then he'd encountered Mick – then Mike – Jagger and Keith Richard after an impromptu performance sitting in with Alexis Korner and Cyril Davis. His ability to duplicate 'Dust My Blues' live with all the slide guitar embellishments had the pair well impressed and they were even more impressed, if a little shocked probably, by Jones' casual disclosure that he had two illegitimate children by different girls and the second one was living with him in London but he was just living off her money, man you know what I mean. Actually Jagger and Richard were much less worldly and didn't know exactly what he meant but they nodded because they got the gist right enough and because they definitely wanted in. From that moment on the Rolling Stones were born and the sixties started really swinging.

To the vital Rolling Stones equation, Jones brought with him a brawny Glaswegian straight named Ian Stewart, a hard worker who played strong piano and who Brian Jones would soon enough sell out and betray. Together this four piece (Jagger moonlighting at the London School of Economics) rehearsed and with Keith and Brian living in now mythic squalor over in Chelsea's Edith Grove, the sound was fused: Keith Richard's primordial gut riffing – the very churn of

*Jones paraded in fancy dress – lavender suede boots, day-glo sequins and costume jewellery.*

sedition itself – over which Brian Jones' guitar agitated, investing the blending with a seething malicious energy that was his and his alone. This and the maniacally assertive force of his personality made him the leader of the Rolling Stones at this time and it was a position he was to connive his way into maintaining only until the other members could be bothered to dispute it. He did himself no favours here because as the others, Jagger, Richard, stone-faced Charlie Watts and Bill Wyman, were soon to discover, behind the easy charm and china-cat precocity lay a shallow, maladjusted temperament. As a leader he was just hopeless: playing one off against another ceaselessly but always ineptly. When he went behind the others' backs to demand an extra £5 per gig for himself the jig was well and truly up but it was over anyway the minute sixties mega-spiv Andrew Oldham, nineteen and defiantly amoral, had laid eyes on the Stones.

That Oldham and Jones never got on is a little ironic because the hype which Oldham successfully sold the world – the Rolling Stones-are-not-just-another-group-they're-a-way-of-life – was totally dependent on the infuriating dimension that Brian Jones gave the whole endeavour; because the fans instinctively guessed that the 'way of life' being intimated here was the one Brian Jones more than any other appeared to be leading on a day-to-day basis. Anyway, although they initially conspired together (Ian Stewart's expulsion was their first piece of smarmy manoeuvring), they hated each other, and Oldham wanted him out even before 'Satisfaction', probably pretty much from day one. For, wreckless and beautiful Jones may have been, but Oldham's showbiz instincts told him that there was no staying power in a Brian Jones. Quite simply he was too much of a pain in the ass, one big problem. If he could have written songs, if he could have focussed and articulated his torment instead of letting it turn him into a self-indulgent brattish malcontent, then things might have been different. But when Oldham successfully instigated Rolling Stones original material from the hard-working and more disciplined Jagger and Richard, Brian Jones' careerist and artistic pipe-dreams of controlling the Stones framework just evaporated overnight.

In things that really mattered, he was always his own worst enemy anyway. His natural talents he squandered, as simple as that. After the outset of 1965 he rarely, if ever, played guitar on a Rolling Stones record again, forcing Keith Richard to double-track ceaselessly in the studio because Jones was too

*Jones with the reckless Anita Pallenberg, the woman who left him for Keith Richard.*

out of it, or because he was ill and just didn't feel like turning up. On the ceaseless treadmill of a gruelling world tour schedule through '65 and '66 Brian Jones was always the weak link. It didn't matter so much that he couldn't – or wouldn't play his prescribed parts – (he'd defiantly vamp the riff of Popeye the Sailorman during 'Satisfaction', for example) because at Rolling Stones concerts in the sixties all definition was lost under a sulphurous wall of frantic strumming and screaming anyway. But when he physically couldn't make it onstage – he was always being hospitalized for 'nervous breakdowns', for taking too many drugs or because he'd broken his hand beating up a girl-

friend – the other four hated and resented him. Not without reason, one feels.

Also he was always hanging out with the rivals. He was a bit of a groupie really in that way though they all treated him as an equal. The Beatles regarded him with genuine affection (they even recorded with him), Warhol thought he was just 'fabulous' and Dylan was fascinated by him. 'How's yer paranoia meter doin' ', he'd ask Jones, a twisted mass of helpless charm but always delightfully turned-out. And though he'd agonize about his increasing isolation from the other Stones who'd inevitably be working whilst he was out partying with his peers, he was secure, whether he knew it or not, in his capacity for being the kind of star who just has to

*Jones on the balcony of his South Kensington flat after one of the many drug busts.*

'be there' in order to generate the very motions of mystique that culminated in a force like the Rolling Stones transforming itself from an irritant into a national outrage. In his finest photos (and until 1968 there was no such thing as a bad photo of Brian Jones) he looks like a little prince, just exquisite: quite simply he was the quintessential beautiful damned face of the sweet, sick sixties. And he was also the sixties baddest dandy. This was understood everywhere it seems. All the big wheels stepped back when Brian Jones walked into a club, stoned of course, particularly when Anita Pallenberg was in tow. She was the only one he ever really loved, say his friends and certainly she got inside him, tormented him like no other woman he ever got to know because Anita Pallenberg, a north Italian actress, model and full-time swinger, was as wreckless, abandoned and amoral as he was but much tougher. He couldn't stand to be without her for a minute but when he was with her he couldn't stand not to hit her. They looked like twins – eerily beautiful together – and were an item for one ruinously sexy year between the autumn of '66 and spring '67. It was a hell of a fling. And it could only get worse when

Pallenberg left Jones in Tangiers to take off with Keith Richard. 'He'd been behaving disgustingly,' according to the latter. 'I just said "Baby we're getting out of here"'. Another source now opines 'Anita was no fool. She first thought that the real power of the Rolling Stones lay with Brian but after a while she found him to be a weak... She found him pathetic in many ways. Her timing was perfect: she intuitively knew that the real power-base in the Stones – the one strong man – was Keith and she latched onto him. Keith couldn't believe his luck.'

With that it was game, set and match to Jagger-Richard in the psychological war over who meant the most in the Rolling Stones, the war that Brian Jones had obsessively instigated against them in the first place. He had every excuse now to get even more fucked up and did so with dreadful abandon. He'd always taken too many drugs but now his consumption rocketed alarmingly, as he chased after numbing stupefaction with a vengeance. 'I'll never make it to 30,' he'd once confided to Richard, just before their flimsy comradeship was destroyed once and for all by Pallenberg's 'betrayal' and now it was just a matter of time before he fulfilled his own prophecy. When Alexis Korner spotted him at some London 'happening' in the late summer of '67, three months after the break-up with Anita, he was already starting to look hideous... Like a debauched vision of Louis XIV on acid, gone to seed. It was then that I suddenly realized there could be such a thing as an acid casualty'. Not that it was just acid. Tony Sanchez, a minder and dealer for the Stones who divided his time and loyalties between Richard and Jones once described to me the typical start to a day for Brian Jones at that time: 'He'd wake up in the morning, take leapers (speed), cocaine, some morphine, a few tabs

*The Rolling Stones in May 1968, photographed by David Bailey for 'Jumpin' Jack Flash'.*

of acid and maybe some mandrax. Then he'd try to get dressed and end up with, like, a lizard skin boot on one foot and a pink shoe on the other. Then he'd find he couldn't stand up.'

Keith Richard now maintains that Jones' chief drug problem was barbiturates. 'He had an obsession about piercing the capsules so that they'd get into his bloodstream quicker. He knew all these junkie tricks!' Barbs and alcohol combine to cause a lethal, often fatal wooziness. Jones was once spotted in this habitually warped condition attempting to shepherd a similarly blotto Judy Garland out of a club

– talk about the blind leading the blind! He'd been an alcoholic anyway since late 1964. Back then Charlie Watts, to his credit, had cared enough to try and help him but it was all to no avail. Brian Jones never seemed to grasp simple common sense. When he entered a clinic to come to terms with 'stress' and 'nervous fatigue', he took with him all the drugs that had helped put him there in the first place.

This was the essence of his pitiful nature: he'd plough through the dolly birds with a rapacious, often malicious zeal and then agonize fretfully about the loveless life he led, the fact that none of his countless conquests really loved him. Suky Poitier, the girl he picked up with briefly after Pallenberg

absconded from his life and another doomed blonde sixties beauty, once confided that Brian's problem was that 'he basically thought of himself as an utterly useless member of society' and it's this one line that ultimately says more about him than all the psychiatric reports written on Jones in 1968 only to have their contents leaked before he had even been afforded a decent burial. For although he harboured all the flaming arrogant vanity of a peacock, he possessed the sense of self-worth of a hopeless psychotic cripple. Self-love and self-loathing were always in conflict, the latter getting stronger as each blurry barbituate-sodden minute of his life ticked away.

The Stones meanwhile were off being industrious. They were survivors after all, and Brian Jones was not. After the psychedelic folly of 1967 *Satanic Majesties Request* they were back playing their lascivious pagan music again only it was even darker now, more malevolent and assured. Their big comeback in 1968, *Beggar's Banquet* redefined them perfectly. They became 'the greatest rock'n'roll band in the world' instead of 'more than a group, a way of life'. The way of life Brian Jones had represented was being co-opted. He was out of step, out of time but most of all he was just out of it. During the *Beggar's Banquet* sessions, if he turned up at all, Brian Jones would roll up in a feeble, intoxicated state, incapable of being even remotely productive. Pallenberg and Richard were always together now, as thick as thieves and that must have stung deeply. His paranoia meter – 'He was so paranoid by that time he was even too scared to go into a shop to buy cigarettes because he thought anyone behind the counter had to be a plain-clothes cop.' (Sanchez again) – also received a terrible caning from Jagger. 'What can I play?' Jones timidly asked the singer, during one session. 'I don't know, Brian,' Jagger had replied icily, 'What can you play?'

Alexis Korner as an outsider recognized the problems of working with Jones at that time. 'Actually, I thought Mick and Keith were very patient with Brian particularly him being in the state he was in. They didn't broadcast his problems to anyone else, they didn't put him down publicly. They were concerned in their way. And they waited a long time to see if he could recover before starting to consider replacing him.'

By 1969, facing a crippling tax bill, the Stones wanted and needed to tour again. This was the principal reason now for Brian's exclusion because even in the last months of his life when he seemed more settled, less desperate and drugged, he was incapable of physically sustaining a tour. In 1968, after narrowly missing imprisonment for two drug offences, the second of which seems to have been a set-up, he'd eased up and moved out of London to take up residence in A.A. Milne's old Sussex home. It was a gorgeous place apparently and acquaintances remember Brian in the last weeks and months of his life pottering around the grounds just like Milne's Pooh Bear. The most poignant image is Korner's observation of Brian spending hours crouched excitedly rummaging through wardrobes and trunks full of golden trinkets which he'd try on, the finest silks and velvets that he'd stroke, all the sprawling booty of his peacock finery. When Jagger, Richard and Charlie Watts came down to tell him that they already had young Mick Taylor, a new guitar hero waiting in the wings, Jones accepted the news graciously. Only when they departed did he break down, crying softly. A month later, five days after his departure had been made public to the world, he died – death by mis-adventure the coroner stated. Late one evening, his mood buoyed by the mixture of amphetamines, barbs and alcohol he still found himself hopelessly dependent upon, he went swimming in his pool and drowned. There are still several nagging questions hanging over the circumstances of his death – a disquieting feeling that all has still not quite been revealed. For a time conspiracy theories were running riot all over the place but they've never added up to much under scrutiny. Alexis Korner summed up the sorry situation when he said, 'It's true that a lot of people hated Brian and some of them may have wanted him killed. But I genuinely believe it didn't happen that way. Everyone was just waiting for him to do it to himself anyway.'

Dying when he did, frankly, was the best thing that could have happened to Brian Jones. For friends and fans alike, as sick as it sounds, it was a blessing because he was getting fat, losing his looks fast and the image of a fat ugly Brian Jones was simply intolerable. For his girlfriends in a way it was good too for now they could dream about his perfect doomed sexiness without having to confront its often vicious reality. For the Stones of course it was perfect because the dimension that no replacement could ever hope to cover was suddenly filled up by his ghost. I mean everyone knew the Stones were bad but now they were so bad one of them was holding up a tombstone.

For him too, it was the right time. He was certainly intelligent enough to understand that he could never hope to match the impact he'd had as a Rolling Stone, that without their active context he was a has-been. And he died a martyr of sorts – the first major rock death of the sixties superstar era, a whole year before Hendrix and Joplin.

At his funeral a letter written from Jones to his parents during the chaos of his drug busts was read out and its helpless plea 'Don't judge me too harshly' became his epitaph and was duly respected for a while But his absence hasn't made many hearts any the fonder of his memory. 'Quite honestly you won't find many people who genuinely liked Brian' stated Keith Richard in 1988 before launching into a blistering, blasé put-down of his former partner-in-crime. Now twenty years after his death it's the infamous conduct and outrageous narcissism that he's remembered for, the stuff that takes up the lion's share of all those weighty Stones biographies. People duly point to his musical legacy, to little flashpoints of inspiration like the slide guitar on 'Little Red Rooster' (his own favourite) and the percussive modal malignancy of his sitar playing on 'Paint It Black' but really they don't amount to much. What he gave to the Stones was the full force of authentically damned youth. The way he lived informed Jagger and Richard's best songs and when he died, they were robbed of a whole third dimension of meaning, having first become the greatest rock'n'roll band in the world, then 'it's only rock'n'roll', then...well let's just say it's been downhill ever since and leave it like that. 'He was alright, y'know, when he wasn't too out of it or in one of his states,' a friend once told me. 'Brian's real problem... He couldn't feel love, he wasn't capable of feeling real love ever, not even for Anita really. That's why he was such a mess.'

That's it. Poor baby Brian Jones, so twisted, lost and loveless: the spirit that Jim Morrison and Patti Smith have eulogized in public verse, the image that stares out provocatively, disdainfully from all those timeless sixties photographs. He will never grow old.

Who loves you, baby.

# *Janis Joplin*

## 19 January 1943 - 4 October 1970

## by David Dalton

*Janis Joplin was born on 19 January 1943 in Port Arthur, Texas. She began singing country music and blues with a bluegrass band and attended the University of Texas for a while. She joined Big Brother and the Holding Company in San Francisco and, in 1967, she gained rave reviews for her sensational performance at the Monterey Festival. With Albert Grossman as her manager from 1968, her first album of soul blues was highly successful in the US. By the end of 1968, Janis went solo, performing with irregular black groups. In spite of success, she was depressed, using heroin intermittently and drinking heavily. After recording eleven songs with the Full Tilt Boogie Band for her successful, posthumous album* Pearl, *she was found dead of an overdose of heroin on 4 October 1970.*

Two stars emerged out of the Monterey Pop Festival. Janis Joplin and Jimi Hendrix, until then unknown, became not only superstars of rock, but symbols which embodied the aspirations of the psychedelic generation. They were proof of the acid vision of the late sixties – an impossible optimism that believed time could be reversed to the rural funkiness of a simpler era or projected into a utopian future/present where the ugliness, apathy and materialism of the world would be dissolved in a solution of wishes and dreams.

It was a vision Janis and Jimi seemed almost magically equipped to fulfil. Hendrix beamed interstellar signals through his supersonic guitar, while Janis came on with an earthy, elemental raunchiness that had more than a little of the legendary quality of blues belters, riverboat queens and Daisy Mae.

Of all the fantastic impersonations conjured up in that psychedelic summer, Janis's still seems the most fantastic and also the most real. She was as super-real as an acid flash of the Garden of Eden, and as irresistible as R. Crumb's innocent, sensual and nubile giantesses for which she was the model. When *Cashbox* described her as 'a mixture of Leadbelly, a steam engine, Calamity Jane, Bessie Smith, an oil derrick and rotgut bourbon funnelled into the twentieth century somewhere between El Paso and San Francisco,' that was the Janis they were talking about. In the beginning, this self-invention was just an extension of her irrepressible personality but after she became a star it was required of her. The media ate it up, her audiences loved it, and finally even she came to demand it of herself, a broad parody of her real drives and energy. The illusion she created was so perfect that many imagined she really was some sort of Faulkner character, a genuine product of the ruminating, exotic southern landscape that produced Howlin' Wolf and Tennessee Williams.

From the beginning Janis was intent on leading a meteoric life based on romantic, possessed,

*Janis Joplin's style was unique, combining rock, folk, blues and pop.*

*Janis's discovery that she could sing saved her from the rejection she suffered in her teens.*

'Beat' characters. A life of ecstasy, yab-yum orgies, zen pot parties, open-road ramblin' boxcar crazies. A totally fictional life lived according to the laws of fiction. Janis seemed to come full-blown from somewhere else.

The pure products of America, as William Carlos Williams said, go mad, or self-destruct, because the pure essence of America is contradiction. It was the friction of all these irreconcilable opposites rubbing up against each other that made Janis such a powerful presence. If the Combination of the Two is the essence of American character, it is doubly so for Ameri-

can women, and it was typical of Janis that she chose to fuse together classic American types so different in temperament: the neurasthenic Zelda Fitzgerald, the raucous Mae West hooker, Daisy Mae's naïve Yokum, and the Bessie Smith worldly blues biker mama.

Janis had a very luxuriant fantasy life. As a child she painted, sang to herself, and made up stories. This invented world became the basis for the incredible embodiments in her songs. Janis's power to animate was so great she could materialize two-dimensional characters, cartoon characters, and give them life. But those very elements that made her songs so great were what made her own life so impossible to live. Only a saint or a lunatic would live

her life according to the lyrics of a popular song.

Janis was born the eldest of three children in the smoky, humid, oil refinery town of Port Arthur, Texas. She grew up with a background hardly more exotic than any other middle-class, suburban kid in the fifties, passing through a somewhat lumpish childhood into a painful adolescence (her mother once explained her weird dressing as an attempt to hide the fact that she was overweight). Ill at ease in the suffocating atmosphere of Texas in the late fifties, Janis came to hate everything and everyone around

*Janis's raunchy stage act and her voice which fused soul and rock, propelled her to stardom.*

84

her, and her resentment was cruelly returned when she was voted 'Ugliest Man on Campus' at the University of Texas. Then she read about Jack Kerouac and 'all those other degenerate dope-smoking uglies' in *Time* magazine. She made up her mind to become a beatnik and took off for San Francisco. A friend who ran into her at the time described her as a rundown crazy speed freak, 'the kind you see on the street with the little fine polished crescent of dirt around their eyes'. Soon she was reluctantly back in Texas recovering from a heavy addiction to methedrine. Wondering what to do with herself next, the voice that became the compelling force of her life came along and grabbed her

one rainy afternoon while she was singing along with some Odetta records in an abandoned lighthouse.

Janis's first ambition was to be a painter, an Abstract Expressionist painter like those wild men of Art, Pollock and DeKooning, or a crazy mystic like Van Gogh painting his atoms into that cornfield in flames. But the voice told her she was a singer, and she began performing with a bluegrass group called the Waller Creek Boys in an old gas station that had been converted into a country music club. Meanwhile back in San Franciso, rock was gradually replacing folk music and jazz, and homegrown rock groups began experimenting with what was to become the San

Francisco sound. A fellow Texan, Chet Helms, was a key figure in this scene, and when the group he was managing, Big Brother and the Holding Company, began looking for 'a chick singer' he remembered the pudgy little girl with the gravelly voice he'd heard in Austin. He dispatched Travis Rivers on a mission to find her and bring her back.

'Travis just scooped me up,' Janis recalled when asked how her momentous musical career began. 'He said ''Go get your clothes, I think we're going to California.'' Halfway through New Mexico, I realized I'd been conned into Big Brother by this guy who was such a good ball...I was in space city, man, when I got together with the

group for the first time. I'd never sung with electric music and drums and I was scared to death. I got on stage and started singing, whew! what a rush man. All I remember is the sensation – what a gas! the music was boom-boom-boom! and the people were all dancing, and the lights flashin' and I was up there singin' into this microphone and gettin' it on and I dug it so I said ''I think I'll stay boys.'' '

The combination of Big Brother (that band of blond long-haired Injuns with their spacy sounds) and Janis's down-home blues was almost too good to believe. Along with the Grateful Dead, Jefferson Airplane and Country Joe, they formed the nucleus of San Francisco's hierarchy of hip. From here on, Janis's life flashed by breathlessly, a whole lifetime slipping by in four meteoric years, as tragic and intense as any blues lyric. If you could stop the film anywhere along the way, it would have to be there in Panhandle Park 1966 or on one of the high days of San Francisco's psychedelic celebrations. Days like the summer solstice when Janis appears in her purest crystal state, belting out blues from the bed of an old truck carrying the sound equipment. Her hair is triangular with electricity, and she is weighed down by as many bangles as an Ibo bride. Swigging away from a bottle of Southern Comfort, she belts out her gutsy blues like a raunchy mother goose ladling nursery rhymes to groups of ecstatic, stoned kids. At those moments she was the child of San Francisco, and embodied everything in that morning of a new world.

It was after Monterey, Big Brother's high point as a group, that evidence of a strain began to show. Big Brother felt Janis was on a

*Janis's extraordinary life was as tragic and intense as any blues lyric.*

star trip. 'She was into making it, like an Aretha Franklin or Marilyn Monroe,' as Dave Getz, the group's drummer described it, 'and there was no room for us in that scene.' For her part, Janis felt the group was goofing off, not rehearsing enough and satisfied to play their old standards like 'Down On Me' over and over. Worst of all, Janis was being told that Big Brother really was not good enough for her and if she wanted to really make it, the band would have to go. Insecure at the best of times, and feeling an urgency about herself and her music, she finally gave in to her worst fears. A year and a half after Monterey, at a concert for the Family Dog in San Francisco, Big Brother and Janis parted company.

The two albums they recorded together still seem like the best souvenir of that time – the all-night parties for the Hell's Angels at the Avalon Ballroom, and endless afternoons playing in Golden Gate Park. Even the shoddily produced first album, *Big Brother And The Holding Company*, now seems evocative simply *because* of its primitive quality. And *Cheap Thrills*, with its Crumb cartoon cover featuring a cyclopic Jim Gurley tripping in the desert, talking 2s, and a Hell's Angels' seal of approval perfectly expressing its appetizing table of contents: 'Piece Of My Heart', 'Turtle Blues', 'Combination Of The Two' and 'Ball And Chain'.

'Piece Of My Heart' and 'Ball And Chain' are little cinematic epics, Zap grand opera – a whole narrative bursting the membrane between outer and inner, a condensed history of American vocal styles and mythic transportation. In 'Summertime' Janis's voice descends on this hazy Shubert Alley blues like an alligator at a Baptist picnic. Janis's singing was her own expressionist soundtrack to the ongoing animated movie she saw projected in

her head. Her attack on a song was a kind of vocal Abstract Expressionism. The flourishes and excesses that people said were too much in her singing are accepted, for instance, as the essence of Action Painting. Janis's feral howls, vowel-grinding groans and other sonic effects can be seen as a gestural language like the drips, gashes of colour and impasto of painting.

Big Brother wasn't the greatest band in the world, but together with Janis they formed a family, and the hip community and San Francisco in particular never forgave Janis for splitting it up. They could not see that Janis was looking for a way for her music to develop. She especially idolized Otis Redding's piston-like gutsy precision, and wanted to fuse herself onto that mainstream of soul music. Early in 1969 she began assembling a group with the standard soul horn section that turned out to be a pale imitation of Detroit and Memphis R&B bands. Her second band was so anonymous that it never even got named, although Janis, putting on her critics, jokingly referred to them as the Joplinaires.

Where Big Brother had been a unit, the second band was merely a professional back-up band. They failed to impress even the soul musicians they modelled themselves on. The disastrous reception the group received at the Memphis Sound Party in December of 1969 was typical of reactions to Janis's new group. While Janis was with Big Brother she had the San Francisco seal of approval, and in the hip music community they could do no wrong. Now she was a lone target. The very things that had made her such a sensation at Monterey were used against her. 'She doesn't so much sing a song as strangle it to death right before your eyes,' wrote one critic.

If the faceless line-up was never a group, most of them were competent musicians, and the one album

that came out of her association with them, *I Got Dem Ol' Kozmic Blues Mama*, produced a great hit single in 'Try', as well as the incredible 'Work Me Lord' and a jazz-tinged pathetic self-portrait in 'Little Girl Blue'. A year after they first got together, Janis disbanded the new group and disappeared into the jungles of Brazil with a man she referred to as 'a huge bear of a beatnik'. She wanted to recuperate from a life of touring and try to kick a heavy heroin habit she had contracted while with Big Brother.

When Janis died alone in her motel room in Los Angeles on 4 October 1970 at the age of 27, just a few months after Hendrix had choked to death on his own vomit in a similar drug 'suicide', it seemed as if the lid had been sealed forever on the millennial dreams of the psychedelic era. Her death seemed totally incomprehensible. She had just completed recording what is probably the best album of her career, *Pearl*, had a hit single in the charts with 'Me And Bobby McGee', had finally got together the ideal group in the Full Tilt Boogie Band, found the love of her life and was planning to get married. What more could she have wanted?

And yet that was always the problem with Janis. As her old friend Country Joe MacDonald said, 'Her game was running out because her dreams were coming true.' It was a paradox Janis understood only too well but somehow that only made it worse. She colourfully referred to this sorry state of affairs as the Great Saturday Night Swindle; she felt that this cosmic con trick was at the core of everything, the reason the blues will always be around.

'You got to remember to spell it with a ''K'', Honey,' she said about her own great 'Kozmic Blues', the song that seemed to sum up the whole predicament for her. 'It's too down and lonely a trip to be taken seriously, it has to be a Crumb car-

*Janis revelled in the wild-girl image that both fans and media demanded of her.*

toon like ''White Man'', I mean it'd have to be, but the Kozmic Blues just means that, no matter what you do man, you get shot down anyway...

'I remember when I was a kid they always told me, ''Oh you're unhappy because you're going through adolescence, as soon as you get to be a grown-up everything's going to be cool.'' I really believed that you know. Or as soon as you meet the right man or if only I could get laid, if only I could get a little bread together, everything will be all right. And then one day I finally realized that it ain't all right and it ain't never gonna be all right, there's always something that's gonna go wrong.'

Janis lived a life as intense as any blues lyric. In the end, her body too confused to go on, her colossal optimism continually disappointed, she collapsed. She had extended the blues, it seemed, as far as it could go, and then followed its doom-laden notes, still grasping like some giant child for the dreams of sensuality and ecstasy.

# John Lennon

## 9 October 1940 - 8 December 1980

## by Philip Norman

*John Lennon was born in Liverpool on 9 October 1940. He formed his first group in 1960, out of which grew the Beatles. The Beatles first Number 1 hit was in 1963, one of 150 songs produced by the Lennon and McCartney songwriting partnership. Lennon married student sweetheart Cynthia Powell in 1962 and their son Julian was born a year later. But in 1966 he met the notorious Yoko Ono and by 1968 his marriage to Cynthia was over. He married Yoko Ono in 1969, a move which was to draw him further away from the Beatles, until the group finally split up in 1970. Lennon went on to make several solo albums and moved to New York in 1972. Always a controversial figure, Lennon was shot dead in the street outside his New York apartment by Mark Chapman on 8 December 1980.*

One of the more persistent myths surrounding John Lennon is that he was brought up in poverty by working-class Liverpool parents. It makes a too-neat antithesis to imagine the musician who jolted, entranced and exasperated his generation starting life as a grimy, northern street urchin. In fact, he grew up in a respectable suburb, in a mock-Tudor villa near a golf course. His school, Quarry Bank Grammar, had uniforms, a Latin

motto (*Ex Hic Metallo Virtutem*), and masters in gowns who could administer canings.

The Quarry Bank punishment book between 1952 and 1956 records the diverse crimes for which J. W. (for Winston) Lennon and his crony, Pete Shotton, were beaten and these fit the later persona more comfortably: 'Throwing blackboard duster out of window; cutting class and going awol; gambling on school field during house match.'

Mimi Smith, the aunt who educated John and whom he resembled

in his not inconsiderable virtues, remembers those lawless school days. 'I used to dread it when the phone went at ten o'clock in the mornings. ''Hallo Mrs Smith, it's the secretary, Quarry Bank, here.'' ''Oh Lord,'' I'd think, ''what's he done now?''.'

As John himself was to remark 15 years later, when the world's adoration had turned to puzzled resentment: 'People try and put me into their bag. They expect me to be lovable, but I was never that. Even at school I was just Lennon.'

John Lennon was born on 9 October 1940, during one of the fiercest German air raids on Liverpool Docks. His father, Freddy, an itinerant ship's steward, had vanished overseas months earlier. His mother, Julia, a frivolous, pretty girl, entrusted John to her elder sister, Mary – Mimi – whose husband George ran a small dairy farm. To John, Mimi spelled rules and discipline: his mother was more like an elder sister. He loved her easy-going ways and the jokes she played to amuse him and his friends. She would answer the door wearing knickers on her head, or

*Lennon was always the most unconventional and original member of the Beatles.*

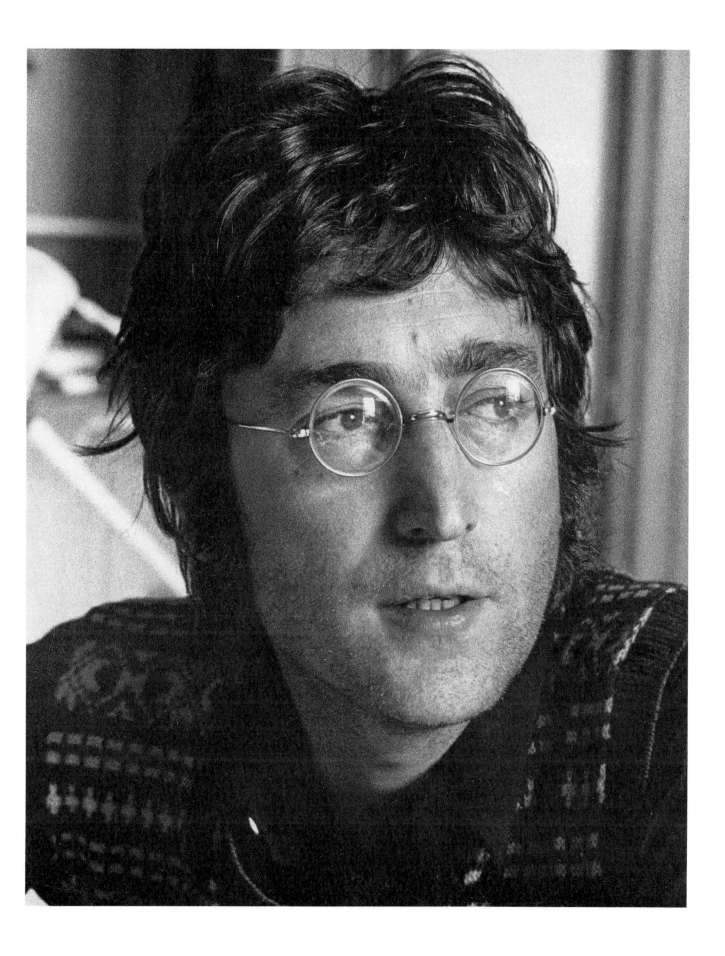

with spectacles that had no glass in the frames.

Though Mimi strove conscientiously with him, John proved to be exactly like Julia. He never cared what he said or did. By the age of eight, he was an incorrigible truant, leader of a gang which terrorized sedate Woolton, shoplifting, breaking windows, even trying to derail trams. At school he stayed resolutely bottom of his class even though he loved reading, writing and drawing.

In 1956, 16-year-old John Lennon, together with every British boy of his age, was galvanized by a jagged, uproarious American noise. Rock'n'roll music, the white man's version of negro rhythm and blues, sung by a palpitating, silver-torsoed young bruiser named Elvis Presley, gave teenage rebellion its first anthems and its first knee-trembling god. When John heard Elvis's 'Heartbreak Hotel' only one Liverpudlian word could describe him: he was 'lost'.

A tight-lipped Aunt Mimi bought him a £12 Spanish guitar. With a group of friends he formed a skiffle group called the Quarry Men, and became its undisputed leader. Since he could not remember song lyrics, he took to making up his own. On 6 July 1957, Paul McCartney cycled over from Allerton at the invitation of a class-mate, also a member of the group. The songwriting partnership destined to outshine any in history was formed in St Peter's Parish Hall, Woolton, when 16-year-old John, smelling strongly of illicitly consumed beer, looked over Paul's shoulder to copy the guitar chords he was playing.

John and Paul became friends, although their temperaments were dissimilar. What drew them close was their passion for music – for Elvis and Buddy Holly, and for the more raffish black R&B music brought home by stewards on the transatlantic liners.

On leaving school, John attended Liverpool Art College where a friend, Stu Sutcliffe, stimulated John to draw and paint and introduced him to a personal style far removed from the embryonic Ted that Lennon was turning into. Stuart Sutcliffe was invited to join John's group, while a youth named George Harrison – castigated at first by John for 'tagging along' also

*The Beatles in 1962. Left to right: Ringo Starr, Paul McCartney, John Lennon and George Harrison.*

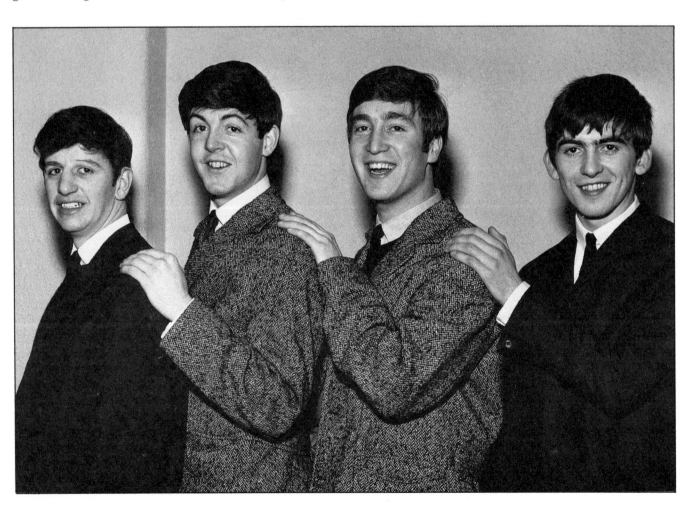

found his way into the group.

That summer, while crossing the road near Mimi's house, John's mother Julia was knocked down by a car and killed. John, though he showed little emotion at the time, carried the scar of Julia's death for the rest of his life, and into memorable, but incomplete, solo songs.

In 1960, the still-unnamed John Lennon group made several important acquisitions. The first was a manager, Allan Williams, in whose coffee bar John would idle away his student terms. The second, sorely-needed, was a drummer, Tommy Moore. The third was a name. They wanted something with a chirpy sound like Buddy Holly's Crick-

*John had a mischievous and outrageous sense of humour which often got him into trouble.*

ets. Stu Sutcliffe suggested 'beetles' and John, punningly, changed it to 'beat-les'.

Allan Williams, though sometimes erratic, got the group their first work as professional musicians. In May 1960, they toured Scotland as backing group for a singer named Johnny Gentle. Shortly afterwards, Williams managed a more dazzling coup. The Beatles were sent to Hamburg to play at a club in the St Pauli red-light district. Lacking a drummer again, they hurriedly recruited Pete Best, a handsome if taciturn boy whose mother ran a small coffee club in suburban Liverpool.

Hamburg's Reeperbahn proved anything but glamorous. The five Beatles, John, Paul, George, Stu and Pete, lived in squalor behind

the screen of a small cinema. For five or six hours each night, with only minimal breaks, they blasted out their music before the indifferent eyes of whores and clients at a downstairs club called the Indra. It was in an effort to enthuse this audience that John would launch into writhing parodies of rock'n'roll idols like Elvis and Gene Vincent. By day, he was hardly less outrageous. He would loll around the Grosse Freiheit in his underwear, or build effigies of Christ to shock the Sunday morning churchgoers. At length even the Reeperbahn demurred. The group broke up after a fire at their lodgings and the deportation of George Harrison, Paul McCartney and Pete Best.

They reassembled in Liverpool to play at their most celebrated venue,

*Lennon with His Holiness the Maharishi Mahesh Yogi on the train for Bangor in 1967.*

the Cavern Club. This was nothing grander than a brick cellar under warehouses in Matthew Street, with walls streaming with condensation and dead rats under the stage. The Beatles performed at lunchtime, in the evening, sometimes all night, employing the vast repertoire and almost subconscious unity they had acquired in Hamburg. It was at the Cavern one lunchtime, by one of the vast coincidences that were to occur throughout their career, that Brian Epstein stumbled on them.

There seemed no logical reason why Epstein, the son of a Liverpool Jewish family well established in the retail trade, should suddenly decide to manage a group of down-at-heel Liverpool rockers. As director of his family's NEMS record shop in Whitechapel, he already ran a large profitable business; his taste in music, like his appearance, was deeply conservative. Even though only 27, he was worlds apart from the fans who queued daily among the fruit boxes in Matthew Street.

But Brian, unknown to his employees, his close friends, even his family, was also a homosexual with a barely-subdued passion for drama, even danger, in his clandestine affairs. His interest in the Beatles centred, not on their musical talent – though he recognized

that – but on the boy in front whose toughness and crudeness were relentlessly affected. That first day at the Cavern, Brian Epstein fell hopelessly in love with John Lennon.

On the strength of his inadmissible adoration, Brian became a manager unprecedented in the pop music business for flair and taste, and also decency and square-dealing. He transformed the Beatles in a few months from scuffling stage-arabs to smart little bandsmen in high-buttoned suits. John, though he railed bitterly against this 'selling out' went along with the common vote, just as he was to do again and again in the future. At this point, he came perilously near to quitting the Beatles and joining his friend Stu Sutcliffe, who had left to study art in Hamburg under Eduardo Paolozzi. Stu's death from a brain haemorrhage, on the eve of the Beatles' breakthrough, opened a second, secret void in John Lennon's life.

Brian, meanwhile, after a discouraging round of the London record companies, managed to audition the Beatles with Parlophone, an obscure label in the EMI group, whose solitary 'A&R' man, George Martin, was best known for making comedy records. Martin signed the Beatles at a royalty of a penny per record, and, after some misgivings, allowed them to make their debut with a Lennon-McCartney composition, 'Love Me Do'. On the eve of the session, their drummer Pete Best found himself ousted in favour of a frail, melancholy boy named Ringo Starr, whom the others enticed from a rival Mersey group.

'Love Me Do' rose no higher than 17th in the British Top 20. It was the Beatles' follow-up, 'Please Please Me', Number 1 in March, 1963, which stamped their outlandish new sound and took over a heavily snowbound Britain. From

*In 1966 John met the already notorious Yoko Ono and was immediately drawn to her.*

the very beginning their sound and their appearance seemed to focus on the chirpy, anarchic figure, John Lennon; an anti-star, even when stardom came, who told reporters that his heroes were Chuck Berry and Ingmar Bergman, his favourite film star was Juliette Greco and his type of car was a bus.

Beatlemania, the *Daily Mirror*'s coinage for that madness which gripped Britain initially, and then the whole western hemisphere, owed its genesis to a Fleet Street trick. The papers sensed their readership to be sated with the dingy adventures of John Profumo, Christine Keeler and the tottering Macmillan government. But the mania, once noticed, proved bigger than any front page. A whole generation, left intact by 20 years'

peace, unstiffened by National Service, with fortunes to fritter on its youthful pleasures, established the unsteady decade in one great, shivering scream for John, Paul, George and Ringo.

As simple freaks of fame, however vast, the Beatles would have quickly expired. They endured because they were like no teenage idols before them: clear-headed, sharp-witted, above all endowed with the flash-quick repartee of their native Liverpool. Though the repartee was communal, somehow it was John who grunted out the devastating one-liners that are still quoted today. To George Martin, he was like a precocious child, scarcely conscious of the joltingly funny things he said.

America succumbed to Beatlemania in February 1964, thanks to a still larger and more eerie coincidence. The previous November, on

the very day the Beatles' second LP was released, President Kennedy was assassinated in Dallas. The deep-seated American jingoism which had always barred immigrant popular music now dissolved in a tremor of self-disgust, resulting in an outward searching which settled on the four British mop tops with almost therapeutic relief.

The Beatles' song 'I Want To Hold Your Hand' bounded into the US Top 10 with sales of 1.5 million copies. The Beatles landed in New York, to a carefully staged welcome which grew to a dementia far exceeding Europe's. When the Beatles appeared, for a pittance, on the Ed Sullivan TV show, they were watched by 70 million people. Billions of dollars were generated by the sale of Beatle merchandise – toys, wigs, clothes and bubble gum. They themselves, thanks to unwise agreements signed by Brian, never

New York. Lennon's US visa expired in 1972 and he began a long battle with the authorities to try and stay in America.

saw a cent of profits literally beyond computation.

In Britain, they were a teenage fad no longer; they were a national treasure. Harold Wilson, that artful socialist newly in power, saw the advantage of reflecting their vast popularity upon his administration and himself. In 1965, his first Honours List awarded each Beatle an M.B.E. John wanted to refuse the honour. But he finally submitted, with only an undone shirt button to signify his distaste, and a marijuana joint puffed surreptitiously in a Buckingham Palace washroom.

By 1965, apart from the awesome sales statistics they represented, John Lennon and Paul McCartney were acknowledged as a songwriting partnership unique in popular music. Few of their 150-odd songs, in fact, were total collaborations. They wrote together only while touring, rattling off a dozen numbers at once as sound-track albums for their films *Help!* and *A Hard Day's Night*. More often, one would write three-quarters of a song, then come to the other for help, with the chorus or 'middle eight'.

The songs they wrote, like the harmonies they sang, derived freshness from a perpetual contest, even clash, of two wholly different minds. John, with his sarcasm, ruthlessly cut back the cloying sweetness to which Paul was often prone. Paul in turn rounded off and honed the lyrics John could not be bothered to finish.

John's was the renegade, the adventurous talent. The emergence of Bob Dylan in the mid-sixties inspired him to break out of simple formula 'Yeah, Yeah' lyrics; to bend his songs around the same punning and surreal word-play that made bestsellers of his two books of

nonsense verse. His words ceased to be teenage *cris de coeur*: they became instead, fragments of current autobiography. 'Norwegian Wood', on the *Rubber Soul* album, was a tale of edgy infidelity to his first wife, Cynthia. 'Nowhere Man' was a self-scourging for his now cosseted life in a mock-Tudor mansion in Surrey's stockbroker belt.

He began to loathe the repressions of his Beatle life – the diplomacy and politeness on which Brian, abetted by Paul, always insisted: the bowing and scraping to mayors and officials. It caused him particular revulsion, as a remorseless mimic of human frailty, when crippled children would be wheeled into the Beatles dressing room to touch them in the hope of healing.

Drugs had been a part of his life since the 'Prellys' he used to gulp down in St Pauli. Drugs became increasingly a means to allay the boredom of limitless self-indulgence – marijuana first, then purple hearts, French blues, cocaine, then LSD, the 'mind drug' with which a dentist friend laced his after-dinner coffee. From the sterility of his outward life, he turned avidly to the grotesque visions which 'acid' provided; he later admitted that he 'ate the stuff', taking in all perhaps 1,000 trips.

He was now visibly splitting away from the Beatles' cosy well-mannered quadrille. In 1966, on the eve of what would be their last concert tour, he said in an interview: 'Christianity will go. It will vanish and shrink. We're more popular than Jesus now...' The assertion – which, typically, John did not deny – provoked anti-Beatle rallies and LP burnings all through the American South. Brian Epstein offered to pay $1 million out of his own pocket rather than expose the Beatles to danger below the Mason-Dixon Line. Brian, in his maternal concern for John, always dreaded what did indeed ultimately happen:

that one night, a fan would walk up, smiling, then pull out a gun.

It was John's bothered spirit, his vagrant and soon fatigued brilliance, which raised the Beatles as dictators over an era which lasted only one year but lingers still as a nostalgic after-glow. In 1967, the lisping insurrection of hippies – Love, Peace and Flower Power – was personified in the Beatle LP, *Sergeant Pepper's Lonely Hearts Club Band*. The concept of a psychedelic panto was Paul's. The stunning visions were John's: 'Lucy In The Sky With Diamonds', drenched in acid sparkle; 'For The Benefit Of Mr Kite', with its acrobats turning 'somersets', lastly, 'A Day In The Life', that strange, tingling elegy leading to a crescendo of symphony orchestras played backwards which John had told the Beatles' producer, George Martin, must be 'a sound like the end of the world'.

Even the critical acclaim for *Sergeant Pepper*, and for 'A Day In The Life' did not satisfy John. He grew impatient with the hippy disciples, encouraged by Dr Timothy Leary, who studied and debated his lyrics like Holy Writ. 'I just shoved some words together, then shoved some sounds on,' he insisted. 'I'm conning people because they give me the freedom to con them.'

1967 was also the year of death, dissolution and false dawn. In August Brian Epstein, a sad victim of drugs, conscience and cruel boys, was found dead at his Belgravia house. The Beatles, led by George Harrison were, that same weekend, undergoing initiation as disciples of Transcendental Meditation under the Maharishi Mahesh Yogi. The holy man giggled, but seemed to give comfort. All four Beatles later went with their women to the Maharishi's Indian Ashram, leaving Neil Aspinall, their faithful road manager, to organize the business corporation which Brian had planned to offset their gargantuan

*John's music worked best when he revealed most about himself and the anguish with the world that inspired the protest albums* Give Peace A Chance *and* Power to the People.

income tax liabilities.

In 1966, at a London gallery, John had met the mildly notorious Japanese 'performance artist' Yoko Ono. She was not beautiful like a Beatle groupie. Her small, unsmiling face floated between clouds of hair, black as her clothes. She talked, and John, to his great surprise, listened raptly. Her views on the nature of art startled and fascinated him. Her fierce

independence jolted him out of his Northern chauvinism; he fell in love with her for her mind. For the next two years, nervously and guiltily, he kept in touch with her.

In 1968, while his wife Cynthia and son Julian were away, he plucked up courage to invite Yoko to the house. They spent all night taping *avant garde* music; it was only when dawn broke that they got around to making love. Later that day, John said to his old friend, Pete Shotton: 'Will you find us a house to live in with Yoko? This is it.'

The Beatles, recording their *Yel-*

low *Submarine* film sound-track album, suddenly found Yoko's black shape in their midst, clinging close to John, as he did to her, breaking a ten-year bond and brotherhood. Although months remained to run, that was the overture to the end: John had discovered a partner he needed more than he needed Paul McCartney.

Meanwhile, the Beatles' Apple enterprise had begun, intending to fritter away only £2 million as a tax loss on clothes, boutiques, a record label, a film company, publishing and Paul's brainchild, the Apple Foundation for the Arts. By late 1968, the fresh green empire was waterlogged with hangers-on gorging drink and meals, lounging on white leather sofas and stealing anything portable. The Beatles could not be bothered to be bosses, nor to delegate executive power: they themselves had been locked in the record studio for eight months, trying to finish the new album that was to eclipse even *Sergeant Pepper*.

The result was the two-volume *White Album*, an audible conflict between Paul's commercial instincts and John's determination to create electronic 'sound poems'. Though hailed as a masterpiece, it was, with some exceptions, an undisciplined mess, its chief virtue the creation of a vacuum in which George Harrison could emerge at last as a credible songwriter and instrumentalist.

In Yoko, a super-charged hustler and implacable showwoman, John found inspiration to do things he had never dreamed of daring. Together they embarked on a programme of consciously ludicrous 'happenings', each drenched in a Beatles' publicity glare – 'sculptures', that were acorns, 'exhibitions' of balloons and rusty bicycles, 'concerts' given from inside paper bags, 'films' of John's penis in close-up. His wedding to Yoko in 1969 was followed by the notorious Bed-in, a week's honeymoon spent in bed at the Amsterdam Hilton to promote world peace.

His arrest for possessing cannabis in 1968 indicated how thin he and his Japanese consort had worn the Establishment's patience. A year earlier, Paul and George had been able to admit with impunity to using LSD. The day John and Yoko appeared in court, Apple released their *Two Virgins* album, the cover of which showed them both with arms entwined, naked. EMI refused to market the record; dealers would sell it only in plain brown wrappers. Another album sleeve showed Yoko in hospital, pale and ravaged after the loss of their first baby, with John camped beside her in a sleeping bag. Though his persecution was self-induced and self-aggravated, there began to be something chivalrous in the way his slight body shielded Yoko's still slighter one.

He announced he was leaving the Beatles after their disastrous *Magical Mystery Tour* film, their chaotic sessions for the *Let It Be* album and their brilliant stop-gap album, *Abbey Road*. As John put it to the others: 'I want a divorce.' He was persuaded to keep silent to enable the Beatles' new manager, Allen Klein, to negotiate a massive royalty increase with their American record company, Capitol.

John kept his word to hush up his resignation. In a strange way, his and Yoko's continuing notoriety served as a camouflage. Late in 1969, he returned his MBE to Buckingham Palace as a protest against the war in Vietnam and Biafran genocide. He espoused the cause of Black Muslims, student activists, anti-apartheid demonstrators and James Hanratty. With a hybrid group, the Plastic Ono Band, he produced songs that showed his gift for creating instant crowd chants. 'Give Peace A Chance', recorded at his Montreal bed-in, became the anthem of disaffected college campuses throughout the world.

Early in 1970, sickened by the mutilation of his music on the *Let It Be* album, Paul McCartney announced his own secession from the Beatles. He did so, not pleasantly, in a self-interview packaged with his solo album, *McCartney*, hinting at his fury against Allen Klein and also at John's escapades with Yoko. John replied to Paul in a song called 'How Do You Sleep?' and a vicious parody of the sleeve of Paul's *Ram* album. In 1971, Paul started legal proceedings to dissolve the partnership, which, in John's mind, had ended three years before.

The Beatles together had given the sixties their shout of youthful optimism. Separately, they seemed to represent what the seventies became: a jumpy, neurotic decade, nail-biting with nostalgia for last year's past, whose music was only plagiarism or parody. In the sixties, things happened. In the seventies, they unhappened.

John, now living with Yoko in New York, made the strongest beginning as a solo musician. His individual albums returned joyfully to his Hamburg and Liverpool rock'n'roll roots: after Primal Scream therapy with Arthur Janov, he produced songs of blunt agony, culled from the threshold of childhood. The multi-layered Sergeant Pepper sound was stripped to a style as plain and confined as a confessional. In October 1971, the drifting flakes of a lone electric keyboard ushered in the song he will be best remembered for, 'Imagine'.

In 1975, he stopped making records. He settled with Yoko, after a brief infidelity, in the Dakota building in New York, devoting himself to buying up the adjacent apartments, looking after his new baby, Sean, and trying to obtain the 'green card' without which, as a convicted drug user, he would be barred from re-entering America if he left.

Massive income still accrued via Apple from his song copyrights. He spent it on impulse buys of estates in Florida and Long Island and a herd of Holstein cattle worth thousands of dollars each. He gave up tobacco, even sugar. He looked on himself as a New Yorker. To him, the city's racy, cosmopolitan feel was an all-night version of his lost Liverpool. He always remembered the excitement of standing at Liverpool's Pier Head, looking up the Mersey and knowing that 'the next place was America'.

Throughout the seventies, as rock music grew duller, the Beatles were a lingering, then a growing force; billion dollar offers were made to them to re-unite. Of all their rumoured second comings, the biggest occurred when Paul McCartney organized a concert in aid of Kampuchean refugees. George and Ringo seemed willing to play but John would not be drawn. At one point, the UN Secretary-General, Kurt Waldheim, was said to have telephoned him on a coded number; but in vain.

Then, in 1980 came his first album for five years, *Double Fantasy*. A letter he and Yoko had written to the American press babbling of angels and prayer aroused deep foreboding. But here, miraculously, was the original John Lennon: older, evidently wiser, yet still as he used to be when amazing years could not amaze him; his emotion bright, his intelligence unimpaired, his honesty, whether crass or heroic, was fierce and incorruptible. His song 'Starting Over' might have been sung in the Abbey Road studios in 1963, with George Martin listening critically, chin on hand.

Not long before his death John had been asking his Aunt Mimi to send him mementoes from childhood – a Royal Worcester dinner service, his Uncle George's photograph, even his Quarry Bank school tie. Once when he telephoned

Mimi, they had a row over the repainting of the bungalow in Bournemouth which he bought for her. 'Damn you, Lennon,' Mimi cried, slamming down the phone. Later it rang again, 'You're not still cross with me, Mimi, are you?' John's voice said anxiously.

*In New York John Lennon tried to escape his fame by retreating into family life.*

On Monday evening 8 December 1980, John Lennon was shot dead outside his own apartment block by a fan, Mark Chapman. Early on Tuesday morning, another trans-Atlantic call came through to Bournemouth. Mimi picked up the phone, thinking the same thought she had since John was nine years old: 'Oh, Lord, what's he done now?'

# Bob Marley

## 6 February 1945 - 11 May 1981

## by Timothy White

*Bob Marley was born on 6 February 1945 to an English father and a Jamaican mother. He made his first single in 1961 and led the Wailers on their formation in 1963. By the early seventies he was introducing a strong Rastafarian element into his compositions. After 1972, the Wailers grew in stature and toured both Britain and the US, popularizing reggae. Following the release of* Natty Dread *in 1974, attention focussed on Marley, establishing him as a cult figure. Both Marley and his wife, Rita, survived an assassination attempt in December 1976 in Jamaica. However, Marley died of a brain tumour in a Miami hospital on 11 May 1981 at the age of 36.*

'Open your eyes and look within
Are you satisfied with the life
   you're living?
We know where we're going
We know where we're from
We're leaving Babylon
We're going to our father's land'
– BOB MARLEY, 'Exodus', 1977

Death took Bob Marley in his sleep on 11 May at the age of 36. It was around noon, just 40 hours since he had flown to a Miami hospital after checking out of Dr Joseph Issels' West German clinic, where he had been treated for lung,

liver and brain cancer. Days earlier, Chris Blackwell, a close friend and head of his record label, Island, had shown Marley a photo of him when he was sixteen, on the day he was married to Rita Anderson. Looking over Blackwell's shoulder, gazing at her slight son as he lay in bed, his dreadlocks gone due to illness, Bob's mother said that he looked the same now as he did back then. 'Once a man and twice a boy,' Chris Blackwell said later. 'That's the way it was.'

The pervasive image of Bob

Marley is that of a gleeful Rasta with a croissant-sized spliff clenched in his teeth, stoned silly and without a care in the world. But, in fact, he was a man with deep religious and political sentiments who rose from destitution to become one of the most influential music figures in the last twenty years. His records have sold in the multimillions and have been covered and/or publicly adored by Eric Clapton, Paul McCartney, Mick Jagger, Linda Ronstadt and Paul Simon, among others. Marley was also incredibly prolific, writing and releasing hundreds of songs that were bootlegged under nearly half as many labels in an equal number of far-flung locales. There was hardly one kid in the Caribbean who did not want to meet, if not *be* Bob Marley.

On the day before his triumphant Madison Square Garden concert in 1979 – a sold-out event which would prove to be a turning point for commercial recognition of reggae in his country – Marley talked about his first record, the solo single 'Judge Not', cut in early 1962. He recalled how excited he was when he sang

*In the last twenty years Bob Marley became one of the most influential music figures in the world.*

*Bob Marley and the Wailers.*

at a talent show in Montego Bay. He was sixteen then, just another poor country boy in the Kingston ghetto of Trench Town who dreamed of hearing his voice blare out of the jukebox. That same year, he did. And less than two years later, Marley would be a founding member of the trio known as the Wailers, harmonizing with boyhood friends Neville O'Rily Livingstone, now known as Bunny Wailer and Winston Herbert McIntosh a.k.a. Peter Tosh. 'I was a skinny child with a *squee-ky* voice,' he said, erupting in the creaking sandpaper cough that was his laugh. 'So skinny, mon! Skinny like a stringy bean!'

Marley was always open in his gratitude to Chris Blackwell, the white Anglo-Jamaican producer and founder of Island who rescued him from the shark-infested Caribbean record industry and staked him through thick and often, thin. Island leased and reissued 'Judge Not' (albeit under the name Robert Marley) in England in 1963, as well as a succession of Wailers singles, but the initial Island album, *Catch A Fire*, didn't appear until 1973.

The first Wailers album to see widespread international distribution, it was not an immediate commercial smash. But critical reaction was overwhelmingly positive, with much praise for the record's hypnotic, sulphurous songs. Intriguingly, the loping, hiccuping stutter-beat that propelled them was the inside-out opposite of funky American R&B tempos. Blackwell and Marley were thrilled with the response, and a long-term alliance was forged.

The Wailers had gone through several maturation processes to arrive at their sophisticated, heavily rock-influenced sound in the seventies and eighties. There was the ska period (1963 to 1966) with producer Clement Dodd; their shaky rock-steady explorations (1967 to 1968) with Leslie Kong on the Beverley's label; the Lee Perry era (1969 to 1972); and the obscure but uniformly excellent material turned out in the late seventies and eighties on Marley's independent Tuff Gong label. (Tuff Gong, incidentally, derives from 'Gong', an old street name of Marley's that was also the nickname of early Rastafarian leader Leonard Howell.)

The Wailers' music was never less than danceable, and Bob assumed the roles of shaman, soothsayer and dance instructor at his concerts, encouraging the audience to fall in step with his lithe rebel's hop as he transformed the proceedings into a mass mesmerization that owed more to a Pentecostal revival or

*For Marley, the first great reggae star, music was his life. He was a Rastafarian, shunning alcohol and meat.*

a Rastafarian meeting than a rock concert.

Marley and the others supplied the religious fervour, but following their juvenile rock-steady meanderings, it was Lee Perry who redirected the group musically and vocally. Marley wrote some of his finest songs ('Duppy Conqueror', 'Small Axe' and 'Brain Washing') with Perry; and while Perry's substandard recording facilities held them back technically, he pushed Bob to eschew his lazy singing style. Marley's approach suddenly became urgent, plaintive, unencumbered by the silly vocal gymnastics that sometimes marred the Wailers' ska and rock-steady singles.

Perry advised the group to minimize its hackneyed falsetto harmonies and work on unobtru-sive backing vocals that would serve as a cushion for sharp, assertive leads. Peter Tosh had an errant baritone he'd long tried to contain, and both Marley's and Bunny Wailer's tenors were fluid but untempered and sloppy. It didn't matter, Perry told them, be genuine and go for the gut. And Perry wasn't obsessed with horns, as were so many other Jamaican producers; he preferred a hard rhythm guitar that was 'cuffed' in sharp counterpoint to the bass, which he allowed to belly to the foreground. The tempo was thud-heavy, volatile and as insistent as a nagging child.

'*This* is how reggae should sound' Perry carped.

Jealousy and internal power plays ultimately plagued the Wailers, and Peter and Bunny departed in 1973 after the follow-up album *Burnin'*, to pursue solo careers. 'Jamaica is a place where you easily build up competition in your mind,' Marley said of the break-up. 'People here

feel like they must fight against me and I must fight against you. Sometimes a guy feels he should do that because he might never have no schoolin' and I went to school, so he feel he must sing some song to wipe me off the market or I should do the same. Jealousy. Suspicion. Anger. Poverty. Competition. We should just get together and create music, but there's too much poverty fuckin' it up. People don't get time to expand their intelligence. Some-times I think the most intelligent people are the poorest – they just want to *eat*.

'God created the earth for us, but people wonder, "Who owns the tree, who owns the ladder, who owns the ganja pipe?" ' He shook his dreadlocks in disgust.

'When the thieves took up with reggae music, mon, they have it made! It's *easy* in Jamaica for any guy who has a few dollars to rent a studio, go in, get a recording, ask the engineer to mix it. The hustlers move in as soon as he's gone into the street; the record goes into stores and Jojo knows nothing about what happened! Jamaicans go slow, everything is "soon come", but if there's one thing Jamaicans rush about, it's making a recordin'!'

When he finished, Bob sat quietly for a moment and then burst out laughing. 'Ahh, nothin' is impor-tant that much, eh?' he said with a bobbing nod and a shrug.

On 5 December 1976, two com-pact cars stormed into Marley's Hope Road compound in King-ston, where the Wailers and the Zap-Pow horns were rehearsing for the upcoming Smile Jamaica concert that was being sponsored by the group and the Jamaican Cultural Ministry. Wielding automatic rifles, at least seven gunmen peppered his home with bullets. Marley's wife was shot as she tried to escape in a car with some of their children and a reporter from the Jamaican

*Daily News*; a bullet lodged itself between her scalp and skull but did not penetrate the bone.

Meanwhile, Marley's manager at the time, Don Taylor, was lying in his own blood at the front of the house. Five bullets had torn into his lower torso and another lacerated Marley's breast near his armpit and then lodged itself in his biceps. Taylor was critically wounded and faced permanent paralysis in his legs, but he recovered fully; Marley was treated at a hospital, released and went on to perform at the music festival. The gunmen were never found, and a motive was never established, although it was presumably political. Jamaica was then undergoing a wave of violence over the future of its Democratic Socialist government, and Marley was seen as being sympathetic to Prime Minister Michael Manley's controversial regime. 'When I decided to do this concert two and a half months ago, there were no politics,' Marley told a crowd estimated at 80,000. 'I just wanted to play for the love of the people.'

At the close of his performance, Bob opened his shirt and rolled up his sleeves to show his wounds. The last thing the audience saw before the reigning king of reggae disappeared into the hills was this spindly man mimicking the two-pistoled, showdown stance of a frontier gunslinger, his head thrown back in triumphant laughter.

Marley's homeland is a one-time slave depot caught between white colonialism and African pride. As the warring native factions in its present independent government deliberate about what is best for their country, they never lose sight of the fact that, until 1962, a Jamaican's opinion was far less important than that of an Englishman. Marley symbolized a bold, hopeful bridge spanning the cultural chasms of Jamaica, and the

third world was galvanized by his denunciations of colonialism and his vivid depictions of ghetto strife, while white listeners were drawn by his passion, his conciliatory codas and the child-like affection in his lulling ballads. Ironically, aspects of Jamaica's racial tensions were reflected in the Marley family tree.

Robert Nesta Marley was born – to the best of his peasant kin's recollections – in the rural parish of St Ann, Jamaica, on 6 February 1945, to 'Captain' Norval Sinclair, a white fiftyish Anglo-Jamaican 'busha' or government-appointed overseer for the rural Crown lands on the island, and his seventeen-year-old Jamaican wife, the former Cedella Malcolm. Marley was efficacious in his ability to straddle his bloodlines. 'He was just like any other little boy, always playful, lovin' and cooperative with his friends,' says Cedella Marley Booker (she remarried in 1963). 'But sometimes he was a little selfish. And he always looked to me like he was hiding his true feelin's.'

Bob was eight years old when his parents separated. His mother decided to give up her tiny grocery store in Alva, a village near the district of Nine Miles, Rhoden Hall, and move to Trench Town. His father died two years later. 'I believe it was malaria,' says Mrs Booker.

In their early days in Kingston, Bob's mother made ends meet by working as a cook or servant. Although the two lived modestly, Mrs Booker, disliking the area's inferior public-school system, struggled to earn enough to send Bob to private institutions.

But she wasn't breaking her back doing other people's wash so her son could boot a soccer ball off the tumbledown walls of Babylon, and as soon as Bob completed grammar school, she insisted he settle on a trade.

'I really didn't choose anything special as a job for him,' she says. 'I

knew men who were doing welding for a livin', and I suggested that he go down to the shop and make himself an apprentice. He hated it. One day he was welding some steel and a piece of metal flew off and got stuck right in the white of his eye, and he had to go to the hospital twice to have it taken out. It caused him terrible pain; it even hurt for him to cry.'

At the time, the Marleys were sharing a roof with best friend Bunny Wailer and his father, Thaddius Livingston. Once his eye healed, Bob convinced his mother that he could make a more comfortable living pursuing a musical career with Bunny. 'Bob wrote little songs, and then he and Bunny would sing them,' his mother says. 'Sometimes I'd teach him a tune like "I'm Going to Lay My Sins Down at the Riverside".'

Bunny says that he constructed a guitar out of 'a bamboo staff, the fine wires from an electric cable and a large sardine can'. He and Bob made do with the crude instrument until Peter Tosh, who lived on nearby West Road, joined in with his battered acoustic guitar. They formed a group and called themselves the Teenagers, the Wailing Rudeboys and then the Wailing Wailers, playing in local 'yards' for tips and eventually in small clubs and talent shows in Kingston theatres.

In 1963, Mrs Booker emigrated to Delaware and moved in with relatives. Because of the expense, Bob stayed behind in the care of Mr Livingston and other friends. Moreover, he was committed to his musical career in Jamaica, since the Wailers had grown, with the guidance of Joe Higgs (half of the popular singing duo Higgs and Wilson) into a group worthy of a recording contract. Mrs Booker sent for her son in 1964, just as the Wailers were establishing a relationship with Studio One, one

*Marley was never really happy outside his native Jamaica where he was a hero of mythic proportions.*

Shift' in the mid-seventies, but the words changed only slightly, the power of one young man's determination shining through as he described his lonely, ass-backward work schedule:

'The sun shall not smite I by day
Nor the moon by night
And everything that I do shall be upful and right …
Working on the night shift.
With the forklift …'

Marley's stay in Delaware reportedly came to an end when the draft board discovered the lean West Indian after he applied for social security. But when asked about his departure, Bob would shrug and maintain that the ultimate impetus for his flight came from a far less mundane quarter.

While asleep at home one afternoon, he had a dream wherein a man attired in khaki and a weathered hat appeared, described himself as an emissary for the deceased Norval Marley and presented Bob with a ring set with a curious black jewel. He awoke from his mystical reverie and described the vision to his mother. She then produced the very ring in the dream, and Marley slipped it on his finger.

But it made him extremely uncomfortable to wear it, and he reasoned that he was being tested by God to ascertain whether he was more interested in personal gain than in spiritual fulfilment. He removed the ring and handed it back to his mother. After he returned to Trench Town, the message of the dream was interpreted further by Mortimo Planno, a Rasta elder and sometime record producer active in the ganja trade.

Bob Marley subsequently embraced the beliefs of the Rastafarians, who take their name from Lij Ras Tafari Makonnen, the given name of Ethiopian Emperor Haile Selassie; they also draw a good deal of their ideology from

of the top three recording outfits on the island, so he asked to remain in Jamaica.

Finally, in February 1966, immediately after his marriage to Rita Anderson, he paid his mother a visit, but he had little use for the United States, and Delaware in particular. By his own admission, 'Everything was too fast, too noisy, too rush-rush.' Nonetheless, he prolonged his stay to earn money to start his own record label back home, and thus put some distance between himself and the predatory producers he and the Wailers were forced to deal with.

Among the jobs he held, under the alias Donald Marley, were a stint as a DuPont lab assistant and a short stretch on the night shift at a warehouse and on the assembly line of a nearby Chrysler plant. The introverted singer made few friends, preferring merely to tolerate the present and fantasize about the future. In his mother's words, he was 'lost without his musician friends'.

At weekends, he lolled around the house, picking out simple melodies on a cheap acoustic guitar and writing lyrics in a little book, a combination diary and songwriting ledger that he guarded judiciously. One of the songs that emerged from that private journal was 'It's Alright', a caustic, exhortatory dance tune he cut in the late sixties for Lee Perry's Jamaican record company, Upsetter.

When Marley first recorded the song, it featured a bouncy, *whoa-whoa* chorus and antagonistic touts of 'Do you like it hot or *cold*?' His temper had cooled by the time he recorded the song as 'Night

Marcus Garvey's back-to-Africa admonishments during the twenties and thirties, as well as from the Coptic and King James Bibles.

Slowly but surely, Marley let his Sam Cooke haircut go to seed, allowing the lengthening tresses to wind themselves into dreadlocks. He shunned alcohol, tobacco, meat, certain predatory species of marine life and food prepared with salt. Anything, in short, that was not *I-tal*, a Rasta term meaning 'pure' or 'natural'. During a 1977 US concert tour to support his *Rastaman Vibration* album, Marley was sitting in a hotel room, reading a newspaper article that ridiculed his patois. He slammed the paper on the table. 'Fucking hell' he raged. 'Tell me, why do they make fun of me? Why do they make fun of rasta?' He began to spew out his frustration with those who mocked his dreadlocks, his dialect, his religion, his heritage. He said that he once gave an autograph to a journalist who then told him he was surprised Marley could write, and that he pointed out errors in a story to another reporter who could not conceal his amazement that this rope-haired Rastafarian knew how to read.

Marley was equally distraught over what he saw as the racism and ignorance of critics who damned his music along thematic lines while making no attempt to investigate its underpinnings, to learn that it was steeped in folklore, in the country maxims he had been raised on, in Rastafarian tenets. But what cut deepest was when some black DJs and station programmers in the United States called his records and those of his colleagues 'jungle music' and 'slave music'.

Still, Bob Marley was one of the most revered figures in the third world. Wherever he travelled in the Caribbean or Africa (and Europe, for that matter), he sparked enormous outpourings of affection and admiration. A hero of mythic proportions in his own country, where he was honoured with a state funeral, Marley had been given a special citation by the United Nations on behalf of third-world nations. And it was no accident that when Rhodesia became the independent state of Zimbabwe the next year, the first words spoken following the order to lower the British flag and raise the new standard were, 'Ladies and gentlemen, Bob Marley and the Wailers!' The government had invited Marley and his band to perform at the ceremony marking the birth of a nation. An inspiration for black freedom fighters the world over, he was mobbed in Nigeria, Gabon and every other African country he played in or visited. When his death was announced, the degree of devastation felt worldwide was incalculable.

Bob Marley believed that he and his loved ones would one day be free of the degradation and moral turpitude of Babylon, a land without borders in which men sin and suffer for it. He was certain that someday he would enter Zion, the promised land where Jah, His Imperial Majesty Haile Selassie I, Power of the Holy Trinity, 225th ruler of the 3000-year-old Ethiopian Empire, Lord of Lords, King of Kings, Heir to the Throne of Solomon, Conquering Lion of the Tribe of Judah, would take his hand. Across time and space they would keep that sacred appointment. You had to envy a man with so profound a faith, and you could not fail to be affected by the fervour of his answer in song to those who claimed that Selassie had died in 1975.

I stood on the other side of the glass in Harry J's Kingston studio on the autumn evening in 1975 when Marley laid down the vocal tracks for 'Jah Live'. As he sang, the crisp mesh of music and testimony grew louder, spiralling upward, higher and higher in a dizzying prosody of tension and release, until its spell was awesome in its psychic grip.

'The truth is an offence, but not a sin!
Is he laugh last, is he who win!
Is a foolish dog barks at a flying bird!
One sheep must learn to respect the shepherd!
Jah live! Selassie lives, chil-dran!
Jah live! Jah-Jah live!

My final encounter with Bob Marley was autumn 1979, the day after his second concert stand at Madison Square Garden. I was unaware of it at the time, but he was about to undergo diagnostic treatment for cancer at New York City's Memorial Sloan-Kettering hospital. Stretched out on the bed at the Essex House, he looked drained, frail and annoyed by the flock of hangers-on that filled the numerous rooms of his suite, guffawing loudly and helping themselves to room service.

The aura of joy that had always surrounded him had begun to dissipate. His payment for the previous night's show arrived, and he looked pensively at the crisp stack of bills as if studying an old gimcrack to see if it still held meaning or should be discarded. He absently passed the money to a band member.

Several months later, I was told how sick Bob was. I began to think back on the pleasurable years I spent immersed in Bob Marley and the Wailers. I remembered hunting through the basement of Daddy Kool Records in London in the winter of 1976. A contact at Island Records had told me it was a particularly good place to locate vintage ska, rock steady and reggae. Sure enough, there were tiers of singles and LPs stacked halfway to the ceiling and spilling out of broken bins. I waded into the confusion and located two of the many treasures I was after; a

*Central Park, 1975. When Bob Marley played, he fired the imagination of thousands.*

copy of 'Simmer Down', the Wailers' first single, which was cut in 1964 for Jamaican producer Clement Dodd's Studio One: the seminal trio was augmented by singers Junior Braithwaite, Beverly Kelso and a woman named Cherry. Singer Joe Higgs had helped them iron out the kinks in their harmonies, and the instrumental backup was provided by various Skatalites. The rudeboy classic, admonishing unruly ghetto youths to control their tempers, was an instant hit.

The second record was the original version of 'Duppy Conqueror', which the Wailers recorded in 1967 while under contract to the Upsetter label. As Peter Tosh once explained to me, 'The Wailers were more interested in ''reality music'' than ''I love you darlin' '' and all that', and the raw, rancorous call to arms that was 'Duppy Conqueror' closed with the challenge, 'Don't try to show off/For I will cut you off/I will take your ass off'. I've never found a band as compelling as the Wailers and a singer who could fire my imagination like Marley.

What I will remember most about Bob Marley is how his music was so much a part of his life. Near the end of our first meeting, in Kingston in 1975, he began to speak about children, how close he felt to them, how their presence always strengthened him and how blessed he was by his own brood.

I told him how I had shuddered when I'd read a story in the Jamaican *Daily News* about the plight of local youngsters who forage through huge trash heaps on Causeway Road outside Kingston for food and clothing.

He nodded slowly and then told me he had recently written a song called 'Children of the Ghetto'. 'When my children are old enough to sing it,' he said, 'I'm gonna record it with them.' ('Children of the Ghetto', since retitled 'Children Playing in the Street', was released on Tuff Gong in 1979 by the Melody Makers, a group consisting of Bob and Rita's four children.)

Slumped against the great, gnarled tree beside his house on that sun-splashed day, their father began to talk-sing the lyrics:

'Children playing in the streets
In broken bottles and rubbish heap
Ain't got nothin' to eat
Only sweets dat rot dere teeth
Sitting in the darkness
Searching for the light …
Moma scream, ''Watch that car!''
But hit-and-run man has gone too far.'*

When he was finished, Bob turned away to watch Rita and son Robbie cavorting on the lawn, and he slipped into a trance. He picked up a stick, rolled it in his palms; his arms tensed and he broke the stick in half with a loud *crack*! Then he relaxed, and his lips wrinkled in a weary grin. 'Ahh, Jamaica,' he sighed. 'Where can your people go? I wonder if it's anyplace on this earth.'

I saw his eyes; he knew the answer to that question.

# Ron 'Pigpen' McKernan

## 8 September 1945 - 8 March 1973

## by Ben Fong-Torres

*Pigpen McKernan was born Ronald Charles McKernan on 8 September 1945, in San Bruno, California. After quitting school he began singing and became involved with Jerry Garcia and Bob Weir. The three of them formed the band, Mother McCree's Uptown Jug Champions, (1964-5), with Pigpen on harmonica, piano, guitar and some vocals. Influenced by the Beatles and LSD, the band became the Warlocks and ultimately formed the basis of the Grateful Dead – a name coined in the late sixties. Always a heavy drinker, by 1971 cirrhosis of the liver forced Pigpen to leave the band and on 8 March 1973 he died in California from a stomach haemorrhage.*

The surviving images of Ron McKernan – much better known as Pigpen – are few and severe: he was the singer and keyboard player with the Grateful Dead from its inception until he got too weak. He looked like a Hell's Angel, and numbered many bikers among his friends. He drank heavily and died for it.

Here's what's not so known: in a group of accomplished and serious musicians, he was among the most dedicated, especially to rhythm and blues. He was a blues harmonica player when he met Jerry Garcia

in 1962. After forming a jug band with Garcia's friend Robert Hunter and Bobby Weir, Pigpen came up with the idea of an electric blues band. Which is how, after a couple of changes, Mother McCree's Uptown Jug Champions became the Warlocks, later to become the Grateful Dead.

In a group known for playing under the influence of LSD in many of its earlier gigs – the Dead, after all, started out as house band for the acid tests of Ken Kesey and his Merry Pranksters – Pigpen was the

abstainer. He much preferred cigarettes, cheap wine, and music. 'Music,' he once said, 'is magic. I never took no acid, but I knew that.'

In a group that never acknowledged one member as leader, Pigpen was, in fact, the front man in the Fillmore and Avalon days. While his partners, flying on acid, perfected the concept of the endless jam, Pigpen steered them with his bluesy harp, organ, and voice on 'Midnight Hour', 'Smokestack Lightning' and, most of all, 'Turn On Your Lovelight', the Bobby 'Blue' Bland tune that Pigpen made his own on countless nights and early mornings.

Despite his demeanour, long black hair barely restrained by Indian headbands, black leather jacket festooned with emblems of the Angels, of which he was an honorary member, and a moustache and goatee that added a snarl to his face, he was known as a gentleman. 'He was a warm, lovable cat,' said one friend after his death. 'Unlike many rock and roll stars, he never projected an image of skulking evil.'

Jerry Garcia, recalling his first

*With Jerry Garcia and Bob Weir, McKernan formed the electric blues band that became the Grateful Dead.*

meeting with Pigpen in the early sixties, said 'he was like the Elvis Presley soul and hoodlum kid'. Which is to say that he was a synthesis of his upbringing. Born Ron McKernan on 8 September 1945 in the San Francisco Bay Area, Pigpen was the son of an R&B disc jockey. 'I began singin' at 16,' he said. 'I wasn't in school; I was just goofin'. I'd always been singing along with records. It's what I wanted to do.' He hung out at the Chateau, a nightclub in Palo Alto (home of Stanford University) and met Garcia. After electrifying their jug band, he switched from harp to organ.

Pigpen had been a drinker since the Chateau nights – 'I can tell you everything about the worst rotgut around,' he said – and in 1971, he got sick. Some say it was the heavy dose of acid someone slipped him at the Fillmore East that spring; others say he started dying from depression after his friend Janis Joplin died the previous October. But the medical records show that his liver had deteriorated, and his ulcer was perforated. 'Just all kinds of bum trips,' as Garcia put it, 'from juicing all these years.'

Too weak to go on the road, Pigpen performed sporadically and began working on a solo album. Then, against his doctor's advice, he joined the Dead on their European tour of 1972 and returned with a case of anaemia. His weight shrank from a high of near 200 to 126 pounds, and on 8 March 1973, he died of cirrhosis of the liver.

Pigpen never finished his own album, but, to the end, he sang. Among the many things he left behind was a tape of himself playing a slow gospel piano and singing in a blue shadow of a voice:

*'Pigpen' was a gifted musician but the surviving image of him is of a hard drinking maniac.*

*The Grateful Dead in 1971. Left to right: Pigpen, Jerry Garcia, Bill Kreutzman, Bob Weir, Keith Godchaux and Phil Lesh.*

'Don't make me live in this pain no
longer,
You know I'm gettin' weaker, not
stronger
My poor heart can't stand no
more...
I'll get back somehow
Maybe not tomorrow, but someday
I know someday I'll find someone
Who can ease my pain like you once
done...'

In 1980, Brent Mydland became the Dead's keyboard player, following Tom Constanten and Keith Godchaux. Sitting backstage before a concert in Boulder, Colorado, he talked about Pigpen. 'One of the first few albums I ever bought,' he said, 'was the first Dead album.' That was in 1967, when Mydland was 14. 'I saw them live at the Fillmore West and one thing that stood out was ''Good Morning Little Schoolgirl'' with Pigpen.'

Bob Weir and bassist Phil Lesh, sitting nearby, expressed surprise. Then Weir, who hosted the wake for Pigpen, spoke. 'He's still around someplace,' he said. 'We got him on a ouija board a couple of years ago; there's almost no mistaking it.' The Dead, he recalled were taking a break at a rehearsal. 'We pulled out an old Prankster board. We were all around it, and Pigpen did something that only he could've done: he spelled his middle name the way only he would spell it. We said, 'If you're really Pigpen, what's your middle name?' ' ''Q''... ''U''... ''Y''... ''M''.' Lesh laughed at the memory. Properly spelled, 'quim' is a slang word for a part of a woman's anatomy. Anyway, Weir concluded, 'We put the board away, 'cause everybody got freaked.'

Pigpen had had the last laugh. He'd kept the promise he'd sung in one of his last days, he had got back somehow.

# Keith Moon

## 23 August 1947 - 7 September 1978

## by Greil Marcus

*Keith Moon was born on 23 August 1947 in Wembley, London and he started playing the drums in 1960. After leaving school at sixteen, he soon became replacement drummer of the High Numbers. Renamed the Who and under new management, the band's reputation soared and a succession of hits and tours followed. Moon soon became known as the wild man of rock, as his extravagant, erratic behaviour was evident both on and off stage. He took delight in destructive practical jokes and destroyed countless hotel rooms while on tour. Although known to indulge excessively in drink and drugs, his death from an overdose of sedatives on 7 September 1978 was completely unexpected.*

Keith Moon was not the first rock'n'roll drummer to be celebrated by large numbers of people: thanks to his personality and his doleful eyes, Ringo Starr took that prize. But Moon was the first to be so celebrated *as* a drummer. Right from the beginning, as a seventeen-year-old who could have passed for fifteen without trouble, Moon trashed the limits that the best of his contemporaries – Charlie Watts, Hal Blaine, Kenny Buttrey – instinctively respected. There seemed to be no conscious arrogance or musi-

cal ambition involved: Moon simply didn't recognize those limits. He didn't hear them, so he didn't play them.

Like Buddy Holly, Jackie Wilson, Keith Richard or Peter Townshend – but, more than anyone, like Little Richard – Keith Moon was a natural, a rock'n'roll original, one of a handful of performers who seized possibilities in the music that others had not merely ignored, but had never perceived at all. Listen to Hal Blaine's work on the Ronettes' 'Be My Baby' or Jan and

Dean's 'Dead Man's Curve' – work that directly inspired Moon – and listen to what Moon made of it in 'The Kids Are Alright', 'Anyway Anyhow Anywhere' or 'My Generation': the connection is there, but it is not remotely implicit. There's an inexplicable leap, a missing link, involved – and it's the presence of that missing link that proves Moon's greatness. His triumphs can be described, they can be analysed, but they can't be traced. Like all rock'n'roll originals, Moon sounded as if he came out of nowhere to take over the world.

Clearly, when Keith Moon arrived in 1964 to complete the Who, Roger Daltrey, John Entwistle and Pete Townshend recognized that they had a giant on their hands. Until the release of *The Who Sell Out* in 1967 (when Townshend's visionary epics began to dominate the group's records and demand a quieter, more ethereal sound), the band's best singles and album tracks not only featured Moon, they were built around him. (This was true as well on *The Who Sell Out*'s most powerful cut, 'I Can See for Miles'.)

*Keith Moon was known as the wild man of rock. He joined the Who as drummer soon after the band formed in 1962.*

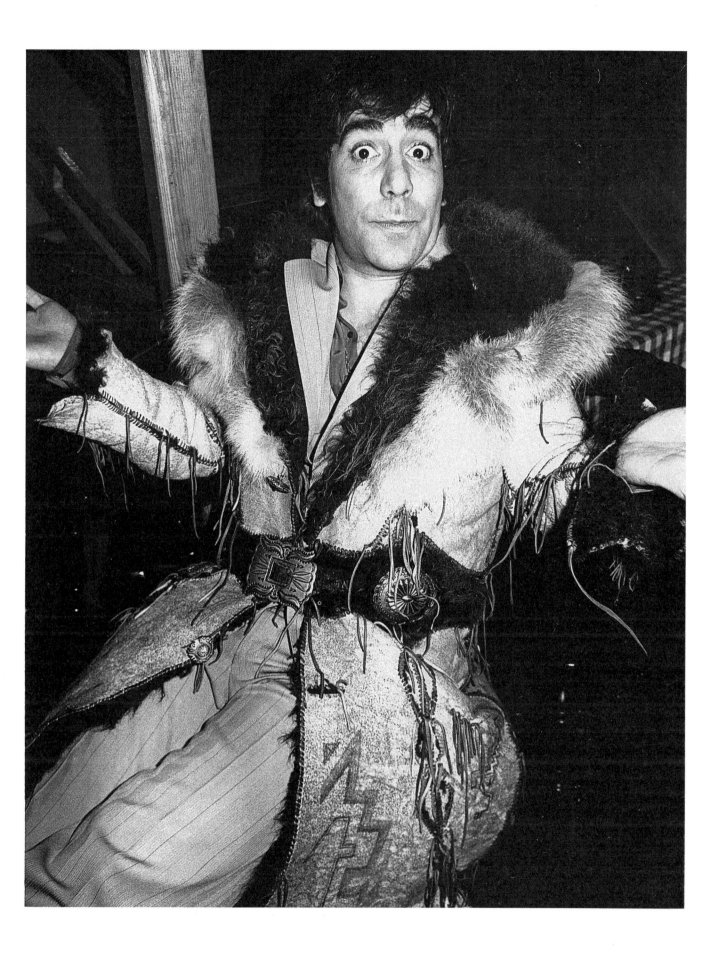

*The Who in 1964. Left to right:*
*Pete Townshend, Keith Moon, Roger Daltrey*
*and John Entwistle.*

As Jon Landau pointed out years ago, it was Moon who played the parts conventionally given over to the lead guitar: on *My Generation*, the Who's first album, Townshend takes his cues from Moon, most often coming down on Moon's licks to emphasize them, when previously the rules of rock'n'roll had always dictated that it be the other way around. Even Townshend's most spectacular early solo, in 'The Kids Are Alright' (criminally cut by three-fourths on all American versions), takes off from patterns Moon establishes early in the song – and which he extends in front of Townshend – before hurling the band out of the instrumental break with one of the most sublime drum rolls in all of rock. 'Happy Jack', a lovely lyric aside, belongs to Moon: even the group vocals are orchestrated around him.

No drummer in a true rock'n'roll band has ever been given – has ever seized, perhaps – as much space and presence as Moon used in those first years, likely because no other drummer has been able to carry the weight. Discussions of Moon have always focussed on his drive, his force, but while the momentum he generated remains untouched, what I now hear in his sound is richness. Although his work was always preternaturally elaborate and complex, the addition of a second drummer by the Allman Brothers or the Grateful Dead should have been taken as something of a joke, and a tame one at that: Moon played like four drummers – he was never busy,

ornamental or meretricious. It was a question of power, surely, but that power had its parts: astonishing timing (Moon's violent punctuation of Daltrey's stutter all through 'My Generation'), unaccompanied loudness (the six tiny shots, heard as two cracks from a rifle, that break up 'I know what it means but – !! – can't explain' on the Who's first single) and, most of all, a profoundly vivid imagination, an ability to hear – and then play – what no one had heard before. And because Moon, a genius if any musician in rock deserves the name, arrived in the Who full grown, he gave the rest of the band, Townshend in particular, the freedom to grow. He was their line to the source.

Moon's influence, of course, was unparalleled, but it was also shallow. After Keith Moon, drumming on rock records became stronger, was mixed higher; kits became bigger, and lots of people knocked their sets around onstage. Moon was an inspiration to countless drummers, but he couldn't really be imitated. Few were good enough to learn from him: Ringo Starr's 'breakthrough' on 'Ticket to Ride' (and for Ringo it was a breakthrough, though for Moon it would have been a collapse) was as far as most could go down his road. Perhaps only Mickey Waller, shaking Rod Stewart's 'Every Picture Tells a Story' to its roots, captured more than a little of Moon's holy brashness: his revolt.

It is really the Who's early years that tell Moon's tale, and it's on the first records that he left his mark. His playing on *Tommy* and *Who's Next* is brilliant, but almost as conventional as the approbation; not many could match what Moon did on those records, but he was not matching himself. Musically, the Who's records were no longer his. Physically and mentally, he was no longer whole.

Today, one hears less of Moon's

*Moon was a dedicated musician with an imaginative and aggressive drumming style.*

sound in rock'n'roll than the muffled flumpf of LA studio drummers. Compared to the humour and the verve of what Moon did on 'I'm a Boy', 'Can't Explain' or 'I Can See for Miles', it is the sound of stupidity, of retreat, of coldness. Keith Moon was a mass of terrible, destructive passion; for a time, he organized it all into his music. When I listen now, the records he left behind make him sound like more than the best drummer in rock'n'roll history, which he quite obviously was. They make him sound like the only one.

*On the set of* The Kids Are Alright *in 1978 just four months before Moon's death.*

# Jim Morrison

## 8 December 1943 - 3 July 1971

## by Jerry Hopkins

*Jim Morrison was born in Florida on 8 December 1943. He majored in film at UCLA, continuing to make films throughout his career. After meeting Ray Manzarek, Morrison became committed to the idea of starting a rock'n'roll band and in 1965 the Doors were formed. Morrison's songs established sex and death motifs which were fundamental to the group's image and commercial success. Their debut in 1967 immediately made them one of the top US bands and Morrison's extravagantly sensual performances attracted wide attention. Despite increasingly successful albums, Morrison's two arrests (1967 and 1969) on charges of 'incitement to riot' and 'indecent exposure', together with an over-indulgence of alcohol and drugs, depressed him. Disillusioned with the music business, Morrison retired to Paris with his girlfriend, and died there of a heart attack on 3 July 1971.*

James Douglas Morrison was born in Melbourne, Florida, on 8 December 1943, the son of a career navy officer. Like so many military children, he and his younger brother and sister found themselves moving round the US frequently, attending schools in New Mexico, Virginia and California. Jim was a cocky, mischievous child, fond of practical

jokes which sometimes bordered on cruelty. For example, he once taped his brother's mouth shut to stifle his laboured night-time breathing, nearly smothering him; at other times he threw rocks at his brother.

He was also a clever artist, a voracious reader with an acute mind and memory, and a fine writer with a dark sense of humour and a fascination for the beat poets and novelists. Probably the book that most influenced him during his formative high school years was Jack Kerouac's *On the Road.*

In college, first at Florida State University, later in the film department of the University of California at Los Angeles (UCLA), Jim absorbed and revelled in the writings and philosophy of Nietzsche, Norman O. Brown and William Blake. While still at UCLA, recalling Blake's line, 'If the doors of perception were cleansed, everything would appear to man as it truly is, infinite,' Jim suggested to a friend that they form a vocal duo called the Doors: Open and Closed.

By now Jim had established himself as an arrogant and volatile personality. Pick any book in the room, he urged friends, open at random and read the first sentence of any chapter and he'd identify the book. And while appearing in a college production of Harold Pinter's absurdist play *The Dumbwaiter*, he was, according to a fellow actor, 'interesting to work with. Every night waiting for the curtain to go up, I had no idea what he was going to do. He was difficult to key on, because he tended to play the role very differently all the time. He wasn't keying on me, or on dialogue, or on any of the traditional

*As lead singer of the Doors, Morrison became an arrogant and volatile personality.*

116

things. There was a constant under-current of apprehension, a feeling that things were on the brink of lost control.'

Jim also impressed his professors. In a course on collective behaviour at Florida State, he and his teacher spent hours discussing Jim's theory that crowds could be 'diagnosed' in much the same way individuals could, and then 'treated', or controlled – a notion Jim would put to great use years later. At UCLA, a short film he produced was regarded poorly, but the head of the film department noted a destructive side to Jim's personality and was drawn to it, 'warming his hands around that fire,' (as another professor put it) 'because of how often that's connected with real talent'.

Although Jim showed some interest in Elvis Presley while at Florida State, and made that corny joke about the Doors as a name for a duo, he displayed no serious interest in singing until after he had graduated from UCLA. In fact, in his early years, family members say he even refused to join the others in Christmas carols.

Through the summer of 1966, Jim lived on a rooftop in Venice, a California beachside community noted for its bohemians – ingesting huge quantities of psychedelic drugs, letting his hair grow, losing thirty pounds in weight and scribbling poems in a notebook (a habit since childhood). Walking along the beach one day, he encountered a fellow film school student, Ray Manzarek, and 'sang' two or three of his poems to him. 'Man, those are the best rock and roll songs I've ever heard,' Ray said. 'Let's start a band and make a million dollars!'

'Exactly what I had in mind,' Jim replied.

Ray already played keyboards in a group with his brother, but the brother didn't take to Jim, so

*The Doors at the Roundhouse. Left to right: John Densmore, Jim Morrison, Robby Krieger and Ray Manzarek.*

he dropped out, to be replaced by guitarist Robbie Krieger, who brought along a drummer named John Densmore. Ray, Robbie and John had met previously at a series of lectures conducted by the Maharishi Mahesh Yogi.

In the months that followed, first in Ray's brother's garage and then on Sunset Boulevard, Ray's classically trained, boogie-woogie keyboards, Robbie's bluesy bottleneck guitar and John's staccato drums were welded to Jim's often dark, sometimes psychedelic, sometimes merely romantic, and always poetic lyrics.

In one of Jim's starkest – and certainly most memorable – early songs, 'The End', Jim angrily killed his father and sexually assaulted his mother. The first time Jim sang that verse, the band was fired from the

legendary Whisky A Go Go Club. Then John and Robbie were arrested for marijuana possession and Jim received his notice to appear for his army examination.

Fortunately for the band, these reversals were temporary. Jim foiled his medical examiners, Robbie and John had the charges dropped and the Doors – who now claimed their name came from Aldous Huxley's drug culture set book *Doors of Perception* – had a recording contract with Elektra, a folk label with a strong desire to crack the burgeoning rock market.

The first album, taking the group's name as its title, and released in the summer of 1967, included a 13-minute-long version of 'The End' and a 7-minute-long version of a song called 'Light My Fire'. Although their first single release was rejected on the marketplace, an abbreviated version of 'Light My Fire' went to Number 1 and the Doors were on their way.

*Morrison's sex symbol image was his own creation and for a while he revelled in it.*

In the two years that followed, Jim Morrison became a major presence in American popular culture, pleasing most critics with his poetic lyrics, pulling the teenyboppers with his tight leather pants and call, to 'Break on through to the other side', befriending radicals with his on-stage arrest in New Haven, Connecticut for haranguing a policeman, and wowing the headline-hungry media with facile interviews: 'We are erotic politicians!' he said. 'I am the Lizard King/I can do anything!'

The result: five million-selling albums in a row, a first in America, a feat equalled elsewhere only by the Beatles; bookings in all the largest stadiums and auditoriums; top television show appearances and a European tour.

Along the way, Jim and his band came to represent the apocalyptic rather than the 'flower power' side of the turbulent sixties. (It was with good reason that Francis Ford Coppola chose to open his film *Apocalypse Now* with pictures of napalm bombings overlaid with Morrison's song 'The End'.) Perhaps better than any other rock star of the period, Morrison also represented the generation gap – insisting that his parents were dead – and the turn against material acquisitiveness to which so many of his peers gave only lip service. Until his death, Morrison lived mainly in cheap motel rooms and seldom owned more than the clothes on his back and a couple of cartons of books.

Most significantly, Morrison and his band led the way in rock theatre,

giving their material visual impact, on stage as well as in some of the most dramatic first video films. For example, in a film of 'Unknown Soldier', Morrison was tied to a post on a beach, gurgling blood at the moment of his execution, while on stage he collapsed so violently, many in the audience thought he'd actually been accidentally electrocuted. In years to come, Alice Cooper, Patti Smith, Bryan Ferry, and most of the Punk generation (notably the Stranglers) owed a lot to Morrison's dramatic flair.

And the lyrics continued to stun, to chill. When Morrison sang 'People are strange when you're a stranger/Faces look ugly when you're alone,' his croon turned into a painful cry. As much as anyone else, he captured the petulance, frustration and revolutionary force of his decade when he screamed, 'We want the world and we want it now!' Touching everyone, he sang, 'The music is your special friend...until the end'. And he gave everyone a look into his own special nightmare when he sang, 'Woke up this morning/Had myself a beer/The future is uncertain/And the end is always near.' Although quintessentially sixties in his role of pampered middle class boy showing off to the masses, Morrison's nihilism foreshadowed the preoccupation of the eighties ('There's a killer on the road...'), and it's no surprise to find almost twenty years later that he is still cited by up-coming rock hopefuls as a formative influence. In fact his own preferred self-image as an intellectual tortured by his own cynicism is at odds with his myth. After all, excessive drinking is a good way to slam the doors of perception shut in your face.

Jim had virtually abandoned the use of drugs by 1969, dabbling in cocaine and snorting heroin only once or twice, to make alcohol his 'high' – or 'low' – of choice. In fact, it seemed that he was trying to out-drink the legends of Dylan Thomas and Brendan Behan to become the American poet inebriate. He hung by his hands from hotel balconies and danced along skyscraper parapets. He drove his own cars into trees and grabbed the steering wheels of his friends' cars while they were driving to test their reactions. He preferred to drink in topless bars and slept wherever night or the final, numbing drink found him.

At the end of the third long interview session I conducted with Morrison for *Rolling Stone*, he said, 'Don't you want to talk about my drinking?'

'Yeah, well, sure,' I said, 'you've got a reputation for...'

Morrison interrupted: '...getting drunk. Well, it's true, all true. Getting drunk is, uh...getting drunk, you're in complete control...up to a point. It's your choice, every time you take a sip. You have a lot of small choices.'

I sat waiting for more. 'It's like,' Morrison said finally, 'I guess it's the difference between suicide and slow capitulation.'

Did Jim really believe he was slowly drinking himself to death and not care because it fulfilled the poetic tradition of which he was so enamoured? Or did he simply, for dramatic effect, choose to suggest that that was his fate?

'What do you mean by that?' I asked.

Morrison laughed easily. 'I don't know, man. Let's go next door and get a drink.'

Following a disastrous concert in Florida in March 1969, the Doors were nearly unemployable. Miami police said Jim had exposed himself and charged him with that offence, as well as open profanity, drunkenness and lewd and lascivious behaviour, the latter filed in reaction to what police called 'simulated oral copulation' of Robbie Krieger's guitar. A million dollars in bookings

*One of the most creative talents of his time, Jim captured the petulant frustration of his decade.*

were cancelled and when finally the Doors were working again, police stood in the wings with arrest warrants, ready to fill in the blanks with the appropriate charges.

Morrison was growing weary. His audiences were coming for a look, not a listen, and when that happens to a musical group, it is the beginning of the end. He had let his beard grow by now, he had replaced the leather with baggy cotton pants, and a paunch hung over his belt. It was as if he were deliberately killing off the image of a sex symbol that only two years before he had tried so hard to create.

He started making short films and privately published two slim volumes of poems left over from his university days. He wrote a screen-

play for MGM with the beat poet and playwright, Michael McClure. Spending more and more time with his longtime companion, Pamela Courson, he actually seemed to be settling down. The binges continued and so did the sporadic, impromptu affairs with other women, but during the winter of 1970-71, he began to talk about getting away – going off to Europe with Pamela for a sabbatical.

The Miami trial seemed, in retrospect, an anti-climax, although at the time the Doors merely thought it 'typical', part of the Establishment's attempt to squelch dissident points of view, which of course included rock'n'roll and the lifestyle the Doors represented. Even though all the witnesses were related to policemen or employed by the city and county that Morrison was being tried by, the jury found him guilty

*In 1971 Jim decided to retire from rock and moved to Paris with his girlfriend Pamela.*

and he was sentenced to *six* months in Florida's dreaded Raiford Prison. (After Morrison's death, the conviction was reversed by a higher court.)

The Doors had a final album in them, named for a poem that soon seemed to be Morrison's farewell to his adopted city, *L.A. Woman*. ('Cops in cars/Topless bars/Never saw a woman so alone!') His voice was damaged by all the cigarettes and alcohol, but the rough-edged, throaty sexiness remained and the poetry was good.

After walking the streets of his tacky but beloved West Hollywood neighbourhood for several days, he and Pamela went to Paris, moving into a large rented flat near the Bastille. The way Pamela remembered it afterwards, or at least the way she reported it, Jim's final days were peaceful and productive...and some of them may have been. The drinking continued, however, and he was having trouble with the writing he thought would come so easily once he had removed himself from Hollywood.

On 2 July 1971, Morrison went out for his final night on the town, watching a Robert Mitchum movie and getting very drunk in a series of his favourite bars. He returned home shortly before midnight, where he found Pamela snorting some heroin. He joined her, overdosing as the two central nervous system depressants came together in a gagging, heart-stopping, mind-crushing jolt. Pamela wrestled her poet into the bathtub, standard first aid for heroin overdoses. It was too late.

Five days later, the Lizard King was buried in the poets' cemetery, Père Lachaise (with Edith Piaf, Oscar Wilde, Chopin, Bizet and dozens more) and it was announced that he died of a heart attack. Many doubted it. They thought he had staged a disappearance, going, perhaps, to North Africa like Arthur Rimbaud, the French poet who had influenced Morrison many years before.

Fourteen years later there were many who still believed Morrison was alive. Surely he was if record sales were any indication; as 'new' records continued to appear – comprised largely of leftover tapes – the old ones continued to sell, even more briskly than they did when Morrison was alive. Several books were published and at least two feature films were, in 1983, being planned, one starring John Travolta.

'Let's just say I was testing the bounds of reality,' Jim told me. 'I was curious to see what would happen. That's all it was: just curiosity.'

Curiosity killed the proverbial cat, they say. But according to his fans, it didn't kill Jim Morrison. He may have insisted during his lifetime that 'No one here gets out alive', but for many he is still a living reality.

# Gram Parsons

## 5 November 1946 - 19 September 1973

## by Bud Scoppa

*Gram Parsons was born Ingram Cecil Conner on 5 November 1947. The son of wealthy liberal parents, he was already singing protest songs in Greenwich Village at sixteen. While attending Harvard in 1965, he formed the International Submarine Band and the beginnings of country rock. After an influential three month spell with the Byrds, he formed the Flying Burrito Brothers, which he left in 1970 to go to Europe with Keith Richard of the Rolling Stones. Here, he achieved his aim to fuse country and rock music on two albums recorded with Emmylou Harris. He died of a drug overdose while rehearsing in the desert outside Los Angeles on 19 September 1973. A week later, in response to the alleged wishes of Parsons himself, his friend and road manager, Phil Kaufman, hijacked his body and burnt it at the Joshua Tree National Monument.*

Fate played one final practical joke on Gram Parsons, a joke he wasn't around to appreciate. This incomparable maverick artist had been determined to win fame for himself and his unorthodox music. Yet he had the ironic distinction of receiving widespread notoriety only after the bizarre circumstances following his death on 19 September 1973 after the bottle – and attendant toxins

– had let him down. Two buddies, remembering a desire he once expressed to have his body cremated in the Joshua Tree desert, stole his coffin and attempted, with only partial success, to carry out that request. So there he was, appreciated in life only by a small, fervent cult, but in death the object of grisly curiosity, another victim of a weird, wired era in Southern California. Then, ten years later came the icing on the cake: a posthumous Grammy nomination. Gram Parsons never had anything

the obvious way.

Songs such as 'Sin City' exemplify Parsons' viewpoint, a jagged intercutting of hellfire and brimstone and hellbent-for-leather. In 'Sin City', the church and the brothel sit side by side, and there's a lot of movement between the two. The central theme of his songs was the innocent Southern boy tossed between the staunch traditions and strict moral code he was born to and the complex, ambiguous modern world. He realized that both are corrupt, but he persevered by keeping a hold on each while believing neither. Lurking in the innards of all those tunes about how the city is full of temptations for a good old boy, and how his girl has left him, lured away by Satan's sweet talk, is Parsons' preoccupation with loss and despair, much more personal and powerful than the banal sentiments that make the songs so provocative at first.

Like contemporaries and spiritual kinsmen Robbie Robertson, Richard Thompson, John Fogerty, and Nick Lowe, Parsons made an apparent retreat from the conventions of con-

*When Parsons joined the Byrds, he led them in their excursion into traditional Country Music.*

temporary rock'n'roll to a simpler, more absolute world. While others were travelling uptown or downtown, musically speaking, Parsons was going out of town altogether – and out of time, as well. He and his kinsmen were lured by a pair of aged, haunted sounds: the dry, dusty twang and its progenitor, the plaid, primal drone. The apparent return to simpler values expressed in the neo-roots music of Parsons and his contemporaries was actually not a manifestation of a conservative's principles or a scholar's scrutiny but a romantic role-player's need for a juicier, more fitting part and a better costume than could be found in the world of Carnaby Street and flower power. So while Thompson jigged into the thatch and thistle, and Robertson enlisted in the Confederate cavalry, Parsons dressed himself in the dudes of an old time country troubadour, but with one difference: his fancy suit was decorated with rhinestoned marijuana leaves. Cultural contradictions notwithstanding, Parsons cut a convincing figure, according to Byrds leader Roger McGuinn, who recalls hiring an ambitious 20-year-old Gram Parsons as a brand new member in 1967.

'We hired a piano player and he turned out to be Parsons...a monster in sheep's clothing. And he exploded out of his sheep's clothing – God, it's George Jones! In a big sequin suit...He took it right into the eye of the hurricane...and Raaaaooow – came out the other side. It was Japanese.'

No matter how accurate McGuinn's recollection is, this lanky young upstart must surely have cut a convincing figure, because not only did he instantly change the Byrds' course – from 'Artificial Energy' to Grand Ole Opry – but he subsequently tweaked the Rolling Stones' Keith Richard and Mick Jagger as they were painting their refracted picture of the American Past: the realm of 'Wild Horses' and 'Sweet Virginia'.

This is apart from the generic influence of Parsons' groundbreaking, if initially obscure band, the Flying Burrito Brothers, who broke rules and honoured traditions simultaneously and with ingenious audacity.

Let's examine the factors that led up to Parsons remarkable entrance on the rock'n'roll scene. The son of wealthy, liberal southern parents, Parsons was born Ingram Cecil Conner in northern Florida and raised between there and southern Georgia, a flat, boggy stretch dominated by the Okeefenokee Swamp.

'I was a misfit from the start,' he said in a 1970 interview. 'I never learned how to play games; it never really impressed me. I don't have a Southern accent like most people from South Georgia do, even though I spent 13 years down there. Everything down there is mushy and red, shifts and bogs, mud ducts. Okeefenokee, by the way, means "Land of the Trembling Earth". Southern people, you know, can talk to Jesus. I could be a preacher if I wanted to. Georgia Peach.'

Thanks to a substantial family inheritance, this Georgia Peach was loaded, and he never lost his fondness for la dolce vita. A born ham, Parsons (he got the name after his mother's remarriage) went from being a front-porch magician to the leader of a teenage Kingston Trio-styled acoustic trio called the Shilos. While attending Harvard, he formed the archetype for his later musical excursions, the International Submarine Band. Safe at Home, the I.S.B.'s lone album (long out of print), is now considered the first 'country-rock' work. Boston inevitably gave way first to New York City, then to Los Angeles, where Parsons joined the Byrds and became the driving force behind the band's excursion into traditional country music, Sweetheart Of The Rodeo.

The album, according to McGuinn, was designed as an evocation of the white southern music of the forties and fifties, with its cornpone religiosity ('The Christian Life') and homespun metaphors of romantic anguish ('You Don't Miss Your Water'), all the time balancing authenticity (Parsons' speciality) and facetiousness (McGuinn's stock in trade). The collaboration seemed made in heaven, but it was shortlived, with Parsons quitting after expressing his condemnation of McGuinn's decision to take the Byrds on a tour of South Africa. They went, nevertheless, with their road manager as a replacement – introducing him onstage as 'Mr Parsons'.

Gram, meanwhile, wasn't pouting. With the artistic momentum of Sweetheart fuelling him, he began readying his dream-band concept, enlisting bass player Chris Ethridge and psychedelic pedal steel guitarist Sneeky Pete Kleinow, and naming the group the Flying Burrito Brothers. After throwing his bass down and storming out of the studio during a Byrds session, original Byrd Chris Hillman also hooked up with Parsons and company. Another former Byrd, drummer Michael Clarke, completed the Burritos roster.

Here's how Parsons described his approach to the Burritos in 1970: 'I try to keep things as simple as possible – we all do – and I think it's worked out for the best in all ways. Inside my own head, I'm sure I'm not involved in any banalities of any sort, musically or otherwise. My foundations are pure ones. I remember when I was a kid playing music, I never gave the consideration to my audience that I do now – now, that's the most important thing to me: touching those people who are watching me. And you just can't expect to wash some people in pure, clean water all the time, you know, a lot of people like junk. And we had to figure out another approach. Our approach is that we're a rock'n'roll band that sounds like a country band.'

The Flying Burrito Brothers took the defiant attitude of the Rolling Stones, then soaked it thoroughly in hillbilly moonshine, and the resulting music was unlike anything before or since. *The Gilded Palace Of Sin*, the Burritos' first album, stands as a masterpiece of both original rock'n'roll and American roots music.

Centred around the doleful nasal harmonies of Parsons and Hillman and the brash, stinging drone of Sneeky Pete's heretical pedal steel, the music of *Gilded Palace* was a revelation, at once timelessly orthodox and eerily alien, like country music recreated in Japan or on the moon. This brave sound was matched by a batch of marvellous songs: among them, 'Sin City', 'Christine's Tune', a sexually and stylistically flip-flopped reworking of Aretha Franklin's R&B hit, 'Do Right Woman', and the dangerously tearful 'Juanita'.

But the Burritos' (and Parsons') romantic extremes are most vividly presented in the album's dual centrepieces, 'Hot Burrito 1' and 'Hot Burrito 2'. The first is suffused with the unbearable vulnerability of Parsons' singing. In the second, pleading heartache ignites into raging anguish. Both of these songs are alive with the stormy fullness of Parsons' vision.

The strength and expressiveness of this new music wasn't lost on countryphiles Mick Jagger and Keith Richard, who endeavoured to write a song in the Parsons mould. 'They sent a master to me of "Wild Horses",' Parsons recalled about his new friends just before the release of their *Sticky Fingers* album. 'You know, I picked up some rock'n'roll from Keith

Richard, and Mick Jagger knows an awful lot about country music. I learned a lot about singing from Mick.

'When the three of us sing together it sounds like Gaelic music – like the Incredible String Band playing at the Palomino or something. We were doing Hank Williams songs and...uh...''Ah wuz *rahdin'* Number *Nahne* in South Carlahna.'' Mick's Southern accent and my English accent. What does it all tell you? It's the same. That's the kind of devils they like to conjure up, if the truth be known. While we sit at the piano – and add the extra ingredient of Richard Penniman. With me and Jagger and Richard, we had Little Richard – Jagger, Parsons, and Richard. Two Georgia Peaches and two skinny English boys. Fun. Drunk. *Drunk*.'

*Burrito Deluxe*, the band's second album, was spotty compared to the first, but it was graced by a hauntingly personal Parsons rendition of 'Wild Horses', in effect his swan song with the band. In early 1970, Gram had a bad motorcycle crack-up, and in its wake he started to down pills in excess of suggested dosages. According to Hillman, he became so spacey and irritable that he was impossible to work with, and the other Burritos had the ironic distinction of canning their visionary founder.

Parsons wasn't finished, though, not by a long shot. After pulling himself together, he located the perfect singing partner, a young woman from the Washington, D.C. area named Emmylou Harris. Stabilized by her pure voice and dignified bearing, Gram recorded a pair of wonderful solo albums, *G.P.* and *Grievous Angel*, each more genteel than the Burritos' work, but still haunted and frayed by the particular devils and angels Parsons inevitably conjured up. Watching the two of them singing, eyes closed in crystalline harmony, around a sin-

*In 1969 Gram Parsons left the Byrds and formed the Flying Burrito Brothers.*

gle microphone during the *Grievous Angels* bus tour gave the observer two overlapping sensations: one, of being in church, the other, of gazing through the window of a lovers' bedroom.

But by the time *Grievous Angel* was released, Gram Parsons was dead. It took Emmylou Harris' emergence as a country star, still singing Parsons' songs, to bring his accomplishments into focus. 'Wild Horses' stands as both eerie prophecy and epitaph.

# Elvis Presley

## 8 January 1935 - 16 August 1977

## by Jerry Hopkins

*Elvis Presley was born on 8 January 1935 in Mississippi. He got his first guitar in 1946 and after moving to Memphis in 1948, he made private recordings while working as an usher and van driver. Managed by 'Colonel' Tom Parker, Elvis signed a recording contract with RCA in 1955. With RCA's wide-scale promotion, Elvis became a sensation with young fans, drawn to his overtly sexy image and he released hit after hit. In 1956 he starred in* Love Me Tender – *the first of his 33 films. After two years' army service, Elvis reappeared with a toned-down image and continued recording to mixed response. His marriage to Priscilla Beaulieu (May 1967) ended in divorce in 1973 and although Elvis's output was still prodigious, he suffered from health and weight problems. He died of a heart attack on 16 August 1977.*

When Elvis Presley appeared on the *The Ed Sullivan Show* he was shown only from the waist up. It was 1956, soon after 'Heartbreak Hotel' had been released, and the lines were already drawn: Elvis was adjudged by parents, teachers and ministers to be a threat, and by this declaration the generation gap was defined.

For many, Elvis was the origi-

nal Fonz, the archetypal greaser or rocker who became a model for a rebellious age. 'They all think I'm a sex maniac,' he told an interviewer at the time, speaking of his critics. 'They're just frustrated old types anyway. I'm just natural.'

Yet Elvis was not a rebel, not really. It was clear he enjoyed the role, but, paradoxically, it was also apparent that he hated it. He was genuinely hurt by the criticism he got in the fifties. It embarrassed him in front of his doting mother, who'd taught him to call everyone

'sir' and 'ma'am', a habit he maintained until his death.

It wasn't surprising, then, when Elvis eventually became a rather bland figure, a patriot willing to gamble his career to serve two years in the army, a loving son who wept openly at his mother's death, a performer who returned to civilian life as a crooner of ballads and opera ('It's Now Or Never' was based on 'O Solo Mio'). He sought approval in established areas, becoming an innocuous actor who ambled good-naturedly through dozens of sappy but wholesome Hollywood musicals, and then went where only the most established stars performed – Las Vegas.

Never was there any rough edge – at least not publicly – a drunken fight, an arrest, a sex sandal, such as was the case in the careers of Sinatra and Brando and most of the younger rock stars of the 1960s. He didn't say he was more popular than Jesus, as John Lennon did; on the contrary Elvis worshipped Jesus openly, and recorded albums of gospel songs. He also took an apolitical stance, refusing to reveal his conservative beliefs for fear

*Elvis began touring as the 'Hillbilly Cat'; by 1956 Presleymania was at an all time high.*

of offending. He generously supported dozens of charities and hundreds of needy individuals.

Thus Elvis became two-dimensional, inoffensive, a slate upon which nearly everyone could scratch his or her fantasy. And it was a slate you could wipe clean afterwards, changing your fantasy at any time, without fear that Elvis would do anything to make it dangerous.

In the 1950s, Elvis seemed to be rebelling against the establishment. in the 1960s – the Hollywood years – he was embraced by the establishment. And as the 1970s began, he *was* the establishment. A lot of people could identify with that kind of success.

Elvis was born 'dirt-poor' – on 8 January 1935 – and he stayed that way for more than 20 years. His mother, Gladys, operated a sewing machine in a shirt factory in Tupelo, Mississippi, a small town equidistant from the fabled Mississippi Delta country and Memphis, Tennessee, the two primary homes of the blues. His father, Vernon, was a sharecropper who served two years on the dreaded Mississippi chain gang for stealing from his employer. As a child, Elvis was shown the scars on his daddy's back, the result of severe beatings by the prison guards.

The Presleys lived in a two-room house, and early photographs of the three taken in front of it make them appear to be typical Depression era farmers in the South. The clothes they wore fit poorly. They looked hungry – probably they were. However, Gladys and Vernon spoiled their only child. Perhaps this was because a twin brother, Jesse Garon Presley, was stillborn. 'There'd-a been one apiece if he'd a lived,' Mrs Presley told friends that day.

By the time Elvis was twelve years old, he was showing a definite interest in singing. He started in a tiny Assembly of God Church

*Elvis shaped the style and attitude of the first rock'n'roll generation.*

near his home, where he was much impressed by the fiery dramatics of the preacher. Years later he would say that was where he got some of the swivel in his hips, as well as his lifelong love of gospel music. Already he was learning to play a cheap guitar that his father bought from his earnings as a milk truck driver, and then, surprised and proud of himself, he won second place in a contest at the County Fair, singing 'Old Shep', a sad ballad about a boy and his dog.

The next year, in 1948, the Presleys moved to Memphis, where they occupied a single room (the bathroom was down the hall), while waiting to get into a more spacious and comfortable government housing project nearby. Mr Presley packed cans of paint in boxes and

Mrs Presley, whose health was failing, worked part-time as a nurse's aide.

Still, she fussed over her son, as a mother bear cossets her only cub. Much to his chagrin, she even insisted upon walking him to the high school he attended. Elvis was teased about that, and also for the way he wore his hair – much longer than the other boys, most of whom favoured crew cuts, and combed into a careful 'ducktail' with pomade. But it was, finally, his music that won him friends, as he played and sang on the school grounds and participated in a school programme.

The details of his discovery and early recording success are part of pop mythology. It's doubtful that anyone interested in rock'n'roll doesn't know he was driving a truck for a small electric company in Memphis when he went into

a private recording studio on his lunch hour to record two songs for his mother. A secretary liked his voice and suggested that her boss record him professionally. Which, in time, he did, using two musicians he had used before, Bill Black on bass, Scotty Moore on guitar.

Rejected by the Grand Ol' Opry, he nonetheless experienced modest success with early recordings on the Sun label that seemed to meld the best of four musical categories: country'n'western (or hillbilly), rhythm'n'blues (called 'race music' in the early 1950s), gospel music and pop (Dean Martin was a personal favourite). The 'new' sound was called 'rockabilly' and Elvis began touring as 'the Hillbilly Cat'.

Along came a former carnival barker, Colonel Tom Parker, who managed a number of country performers. He sweet-talked Elvis' par-

ents into a management contract and managed to sign Elvis to RCA for $35,000, a very large sum in those days. The very first recording session in Nashville produced Elvis's first Number 1 national hit, 'Heartbreak Hotel'.

For two years, Elvis experienced a degree of success that had virtually no precedent. The silent screen star Rudolf Valentino had generated a similar hysteria in the 1920s and Frank Sinatra had excited a generation of bobby-soxers in the 1940s; nonetheless, until the Beatles came along in the mid-sixties, there was nothing like 'Presley-mania'. Before it was over, and Elvis went marching off to serve in the US Army in 1958, he had nine Number 1 singles, four Number 1 albums, had starred in four Hollywood films (*Love Me Tender, Loving You*, the classic *Jailhouse Rock* and probably the best acting vehicle of his career, *King Creole*), and had his face and name on no less than 78 different products. This was the stage that Henry Pleasant was talking about in his book

*The Great American Popular Singers*, when he explained that 'Elvis introduced young white America to the music that had been fermenting in the black subculture since Louis Armstrong's prime. He stimulated in an enormous, young white public an appetite and a readiness for the real thing'.

Everyone predicted that Elvis's star would fade during his military service, especially when it was announced that he would not perform at all during that period, or even record any new material. The Colonel was not stupid, however. He already had dozens of songs on the shelf and while continuing to beat the Presley drum, he programmed their careful release. So when Elvis returned to America from Germany (where he had served with a tank company), it was with great flourish, appearing first on Frank Sinatra's television show, then at two benefit concerts, in Memphis and Honolulu.

The Colonel's next move surprised everyone. Rather than put

his singer back on the road – where he could have continued to great acclaim – he virtually retired him, signing him to a multiple motion picture contract at Hollywood's legendary MGM Studios. There, and elsewhere in Hollywood, Elvis was inaccessible for seven years, during which time he starred in no less than 21 films, an average of three a year. Most were utterly forgettable. Nonetheless, even by the time *Blue Hawaii* was released in 1962, they had become so tailored to the Elvis image – as predictable as the seasons, as pretty as post cards – that they were a category unto themselves.

The plots seemed to be little more than thinly disguised vehicles designed to carry the star into a recording studio to produce another album of songs. Essentially they were all fantasies, totally unrelated to reality, or to anything outside Elvis's by-now sequestered and materialistic world. But it didn't really matter. The soundtrack recordings usually rushed to the top of the charts and young people flocked to his movies (which the Colonel wisely released during the Easter, Summer and Christmas school holidays). Elvis managed to transcend the weak material, becoming in the process the first Hollywood star to be paid a million dollars a picture.

Finally, in 1968, Elvis kicked out. He 'got tired of singing to the guys I beat up in the movies', he said at the time, and when he was approached to do a television special for Christmas, he jumped at it. The Colonel wanted his boy to sing a dozen Christmas songs but this time Elvis ignored his advice. Elvis said no and instead went along with the show's director, who put Elvis in black leather and surrounded him with his old buddies from Memphis. Elvis joked with his old friends and he sang some of the old songs, along with several new ones.

*Elvis on the set of* Follow That Dream *with co-star Pam Ogles.*

He was relaxed. Masculine. Charismatic.

'There is something magical about watching a man who has lost himself find his way back home,' wrote Jon Landau in *Eye* magazine. From then on, Elvis's NBC Christmas Special was referred to as his 'comeback'. As Robert Palmer wrote in *Rolling Stone* not long after Elvis's death, Presley had started off back in the mid-fifties as 'largely a southern phenomenon, but already he was shaping the style and attitude of a younger generation, the first rock'n'roll generation. He would move on to the movies, to Las Vegas, to an increasingly elaborate musical presentation, but he always came back to Memphis, and on stage he always came back to gospel music and rock'n'roll.'

The good Colonel had to admit defeat, especially with movie takings finally dropping, so he accepted an offer to put Elvis back on the public stage, signing a contract for a series of performances in a big hotel in Las Vegas. Again, Elvis was paid record-breaking sums and broke attendance records as well. In February 1970, he went into the enormous Houston Astrodome in Texas and soon after that, back on the road.

For the seven years he had left in life, Elvis *stayed* on the road, performing to sell-out audiences in every major and secondary city in the United States. (He never left the country, in part because of the Colonel's then-secret origins: birth in Holland, an illegal entry into the US in the 1920s.) At the same time he returned to the record charts after an absence, recording such hits as 'Suspicious Minds', 'The Wonder Of You', 'Rags to Riches' and 'Burning Love'.

But at the same time, Elvis was physically and mentally on the ropes. Priscilla Beaulieu, the young wife he had found in Germany and who had moved into his house at the age of 16, divorced him for a

*Elvis always performed from the heart, with soul, but by the early seventies he was overweight and having difficulty getting through his shows.*

karate instructor and took custody of their only child, Lisa Marie. By the early seventies, Elvis was dependent on a number of prescription drugs, ranging from amphetamines to painkillers. Several times he had to be hospitalized to 'detox', although an alternative medical excuse was always found for public consumption. In addition, he suffered from several ailments. His eyes were affected by a mild but bothersome case of glaucoma. A lifelong diet of junk food, mixed with massive eating binges, had resulted in obesity and various stomach and intestinal ills. He had

high blood pressure, back problems; even his feet hurt.

Yet Elvis did nothing by halves. When he craved hamburgers or fried banana sandwiches, he ate them by the sack-full, once sending his private jet from Dallas back to Memphis for an order of burgers to go. When he went shopping, he bought cars and motorcycles and guns and diamond rings by the dozen. Shortly before his death, he acquired a small fleet of airplanes. He always had an entourage, ten to fifteen good ol' country boys who worked for him. With his mother dead, he was spoiled by hired hands, who inevitably came to be called the Memphis Mafia, and even, during a motorcycle period, El's Angels.

Ultimately it was members of this group who blew the whistle on Elvis, revealing a version of the grisly truth in a revolting kiss-and-tell memoir, called *Elvis: What Happened*. But before its publication, his public image remained impeccable, although it was obvious even to the most rapturous fan that Elvis was grossly overweight and having trouble getting through his shows. In 1971 he won the prestigious Bing Crosby Award. In 1972, he filled Madison Square Garden for four shows in a row, breaking all attendance and box office records. In 1973 he did an 'Aloha from Hawaii' satellite television show, reaching more than a billion people, won a Golden Globe for his documentary *Elvis On Tour*, and won his first Grammy (after nearly 50 albums and 90 singles) for his gospel album, *He Touched Me*.

The awards and events came less frequently after that, but came nonetheless as in 1975 when he played to a New Year's Eve crowd of 80,000 in Pontiac, Michigan, walking away with the largest US box office takings of all time. He was named 'Man of the Year' by America's Junior Chamber of Commerce. Even the highway that ran past his palatial Memphis estate was renamed Elvis Presley Boulevard. And still the records sold and sold. Every year with the inevitability of the tides, it was his name that appeared in the *Guinness Book of Records* for selling more phonograph recordings than any other artist in the history of recorded music.

And then, on 16 August 1977, on the eve of another road tour, Elvis died. His doctor said the cause of death was a heart attack. The hospital said it was 'polypharmacy', the cumulative effect of numerous drugs. The autopsy showed there were ten different sedatives and painkillers competing for control of his body that day and together they killed the King. He was 42 years old.

# Otis Redding

## 9 September 1941 - 10 December 1967

## by Simon Frith

*Otis Redding was born on 9 September 1941 in Georgia. His work in 1962 with Johnny Jenkins and the Pinetoppers led to a contract with Stax studios and a hit single – 'Mr Pitiful'. By 1965, Redding was firmly established as the top solo soul singer on Stax. He worked on the road with Booker T and the MGs and Mar-Keys or his protégés, the Bar Kays. But it was not until the 1967 Monterey Pop Festival that he won the respect of rock audiences. The pop-styled 'Dock Of The Bay' proved his biggest hit, but also his epitaph. On 10 December 1967, Redding was killed in a plane crash on his way to a gig in Madison.*

Afterwards, no death seems like an accident. When Otis Redding's plane sank into Lake Monona on 10 December 1967, it was his life that froze. Play his records now and always know how the story will end (and endings give stories their meaning). Redding died (like every other star) 'just when he was about to…'. '(Sittin' On) The Dock Of The Bay' was his biggest-ever hit, and someone convinced me then that the crash wasn't an accident at all, but a mob fix. Redding was expected to go along with certain, er, business practices, and didn't, and was getting too successful for such seedy R&B scams, and so,

chop, to encourage, or rather, discourage the others.

I'm not sure, though, that this makes much sense either. Was Redding going to be that big? That much of a threat to the music biz way of doing things? Play the other favourite fan game: what would have happened to Otis if he had lived? What would he be doing now? Consider the options: playing the uptown clubs with a routine of old hits and the occasional disco comeback (like Wilson Pickett); hovering uneasily between the classy black and classy

white concert halls (like Aretha Franklin); keeping faith with the deep soul circuit – small clubs in small towns, small LPs on small labels (like Z.Z.Hill); being honoured by Bruce Springsteen and Jon Landau with songs, studio time, respect and hardly any sales at all (like Gary US Bonds). When he died Redding was about to be 'the black rock star' but I reckon he was too solid, too fervent for that role. In the line of succession from Sly Stone and Jimi Hendrix to Michael Jackson and Prince, where would Otis have gone? I don't even think anyone listens to his records any more (they're mostly out of print). Think of another common rock fantasy: Redding didn't die at all – he was kidnapped, is recording again. Exciting news? Last year someone discovered unreleased tapes of a 1966 Whisky A Go Go performance which duly came out as *Otis Redding Recorded Live*. Did anyone care? This music – ragged, mannered – seemed, somehow…*dated*. Redding's was a 1960s success story. It's over.

Otis Redding was born in

*Otis Redding expressed above all, the open sound of the sixties – his voice meant hope and movement.*

Dawson, Georgia on 9 September 1941. His father was a minister so he grew up with church music as a weekly routine, but as a high school boy his models were secular stars - local hero Little Richard, heart-throb balladeer Sam Cooke. Redding was a singer and a songwriter, and tried for a style which combined the raw, agitated rock'n'roll of Richard with the cool, tender soulfulness of Cooke. He became a small town personality, fronted high school groups, was recruited by a travelling band, Johnny Jenkins and the Pinetoppers (what happened to them?) as a roadie/vocalist. He sang on occasional records, and when the Pinetoppers were signed up by Atlantic and got to record in the Stax studios in Memphis, Redding recorded a song of his own, 'These Arms of Mine', which sold well enough to get him a Stax/Volt contract too. Over the next couple of years (from 1962-4) he released a series of striking emotional ballads and became (nicknamed Mr Pitiful, after one of his songs) a Sam Cooke-style soul idol. On the cover of *Apollo Saturday Night* (recorded on 16 November 1963, released in 1964) Redding is photographed in shiny suit and quiff. 'As Otis began singing ''Pain In My Heart'',' writes Bob Altshuler in the sleeve notes, 'A half dozen young ladies in the audience almost leapt up on stage. When he reached the line, ''Where can my baby be?'' a pretty young thing sighed, ''Right here''.'

And right there he might have stayed. A successful young R&B singer with a bevy of female followers and a succession of wonderfully emotional records ('That's How Strong My Love Is', 'I've Been Loving You Too Long', 'Try A Little Tenderness') which would have earned him white cult status but no more than that of numerous other great black balladeers (how many rock fans had heard then

*Otis Redding's style combined raw, agitated rock'n'roll with cool, tender soulfulness.*

of James Carr or Johnny Taylor or even Bobby Bland?). But by 1965 white pop tastes were shifting. The Beatles' impact (which, in a sense, marked the rock absorption of the Motown sound) was followed by the rougher, blues inspired sounds of the Rolling Stones and the Who. Conventions of what sounded good shifted from the contrived to the direct, from the neat to the rough, from the studio to the stage. Wilson Pickett's 'In The Midnight Hour' and James Brown's 'Papa's Got A Brand New Bag' defined the disco sound of 1965, and Redding's up-tempo songs ('Respect' most obviously) used the same recording principles of musician (not producer) dominated sessions, on-the-spot arrangement, a sense of immediacy. In 1966 Redding got into the British Top Twenty (much more responsive than the American pop charts to dance floor conventions) with his version of 'My Girl', and in 1967 his performance at the Monterey Pop Festival was as much a revelation to the smart American youth audience as those of Jimi Hendrix and the Who. Later the same year, touring Europe as

part of the Stax/Volt team, he had such an impact that he was voted, remarkably (though this was pre-progressive rock) male vocalist of the year by the readers of *Melody Maker*. He'd become, instant cliché, the King of Soul (to go with the newly-crowned Queen, Aretha Franklin).

An important reason for Redding's sudden rock success was that he'd wanted and planned things that way. He grew up, after all, in a southern youth culture that was being shaken up by the effects of the black and white mix of rock'n'roll (as well as the new economic and political demands of southern progress). Redding's idols, Little Richard and Sam Cooke, were black performers who won white pop fame on their own musical terms – Richard was successful precisely because his rock'n'roll vaudeville hits couldn't be appropriated (or even approximated) by white performers; Cooke retained gospel arrangements, gospel techniques, on even his most syrupy songs. And even before he was a black soul star, Otis Redding himself was a star of the southern college and fraternity circuit – singing his own songs, devel-

When Otis was killed in a plane crash aged only 26 he was about to take the throne of top black performer.

oping his own style, but revelling in an audience which wanted just what he had to give – party music, energy, sex and self-pity and sweat. Redding and Phil Walden, his high school friend turned college promoter turned manager, must *always* have had rock success in mind,

even during the days of the Mr Pitiful tours, and, from this perspective, Redding's hook-up with Atlantic (Stax's distributor) was ideal. Atlantic had been the first R&B company to gauge shifting white youth tastes in the mid-1950s, the rise of rock'n'roll, and under the guidance of producer Jerry Wexler they were the first R&B company to gauge shifting white tastes in the mid-1960s, the rise of rock. Atlantic took Wilson Pickett to the Stax studios to make 'Midnight Hour', Aretha Franklin to Muscle Shoals to make 'I Never Loved A Man', and thus opened up soul music's new sales possibilities. If anyone could cross Otis over, it was Atlantic and, after all, the crucial aspect of his success at Monterey was that he was on the bill in the first place.

Otis Redding deliberately sang to the white rock audience. He covered the Beatles' 'Day Tripper' on his 1965 LP, *Dictionary Of Soul*, and the Stones' 'Satisfaction' on 1966's *Otis Blue*. '(Sittin' On) The Dock Of The Bay', the final breakthrough hit was an archetypal 1967 pop song, a wistful mood piece about San Francisco, the loneliness of the long distance drop-out. One effect of this was the air of self-congratulation that hung around Redding's rock followers – as if he'd come *out* of soul, met their view of progress. Soul fans were less convinced (the Hardy/Laing *Encyclopaedia of Rock*, for example, mutters sourly that Redding's voice 'lacked depth'). Granted, Redding made a classic studio LP, *Otis Blue*, a great concert LP, *Live In Europe*, but the rest of his work was cluttered up with anxiety, strained notes, business, a desperate concern to please.

And yet, and yet. Put these two arguments together and get another one: Otis Redding defined soul for the rock audience (for me) precisely with his manneredness. Far more clearly than, say, James Brown or Ray Charles or Aretha Franklin, he presented us with a set of musical devices, laid them bare, played with them, made us hear soul not as some mysterious quality of feeling (as hypothesized by soul cultists) but as the calculated effect of vocal conventions. I can still remember hearing 'My Girl' for the first time (on Simon Dee's 'Light Programme' show) and suddenly knowing what soul meant (just as I'd understood rock'n'roll after hearing Little Richard ten years or so earlier). 'Inarticulate speech of the heart,' was how Van Morrison put it later, and what Redding did was give voice to such inarticulacy, so that even on 'My Girl', a beautifully crafted Smokey Robinson lyric, Redding is concerned not with what the words can say but with what they can't: 'I've got sunshine on a cloudy day.' True but *not true enough*. For sure since 'My Girl' I've defined my own emotions in soul terms. It's the music I listen to most – not necessarily or even probably Otis Redding's music, but music I can only use because he taught me how to.

A couple of things were involved in this. Most obviously, Redding used a style of vocal improvization which opened up his material, freed him from pop form. He sang around the beat, about the melody; he fluffed harmonies (on 'I've Been Loving You Too Long', for example, Redding couldn't reach the highest notes, sang flat – hence the song's emotional effect). His style depended on the easy assurance of his Stax band (finest backing group ever), driving implacably behind his swoops and hesitations.

But what was at stake here wasn't just a musical style. Redding's approach to singing – making a vocal noise – opened up the question of speech itself, celebrated its possibilities, fought against its constraints. This was partly an effect of Redding's influences – he applied Little Richard's frenzied gabbling to

Sam Cooke's precise tones of feeling and ended up with a sort of vocabulary of desire, a dictionary of soul. Words for Redding weren't simply semantic devices, conventional signs of meaning. They were also always sounds, carried their own aural implications of rhyme and rhythm. His style had something of the joy of baby talk – repetition and experiment, the voice as the vehicle of the body, a form of power: Bam-A-Lam! Bam-A-Loo! You can hear Redding *making* meaning, and it's hard not to grimace and crunch the mouth muscles in sympathy. He constantly stops to savour a vowel, to consider a consonant. No syllable is safe – on 'Down In The Valley', for instance, listen to the way the phrase 'we can't' is transformed into a rhythmic hiccup, and Redding's words thus get put up against non-verbal sounds, placed with cries and shouts and moans.

Redding sang as if he couldn't contain himself. His emotions (simple, mostly – joy or pain) burst through his songs just as in the church tradition from which his style derived, the preacher's awe of God bursts through a well-ordered sermon. But there was something else here too, a more unusual quality that explains, I think, Redding's rock appeal: he was an extraordinarily generous singer. It was as if he sang for us, rehearsed our own declarations of love and loss. Otis may have been a very personal stylist – instantly recognizable – but he was not obviously self-concerned (or self-revealing – for example I had no idea how young he was till he died). He didn't seem to sing about his own emotions but, rather, about the language of his emotions, trying it out, getting it right for the occasion. He became thus (another preacher's role) a source of advice. 'Well, she may be weary, young girls they do get wearied,' begins his greatest song, 'Try A Little

Tenderness', and what's on offer here isn't sexuality as such, but a sort of obsessional romanticism in which sexuality is charged by self-consciousness and so becomes a form of creative expression (and not a source of disruption). Redding's mannerisms – intensity as style – may have been uncool in the terms of soul purism, but they let us, me, into the *secret* of soul (showed me how it worked) at a time when someone like James Brown was still an exotic spectacle.

In the end, I guess, Otis Redding, man of his time (1960s) and place (US New South), believed in the hippie dream; a change was gonna come, but a change of heart, vibes, dignity; a change in people's natural respect for each other. I can't think how he would've dealt with the new black music of the turn of the decade – militant, knowing, city slick, angry – or its later stylization as ghetto and/or middle class hedonism. He was never a groove singer, and if the sounds of the seventies and eighties have been closed (punk thrashing about, caught in an attitude, funk rumbling about, caught in a beat), Redding expressed, perhaps above all, the open sounds of the sixties – his voice (like the Beatles' music) *meant* hope and movement. Maybe (I hope) he died with his 1960s keenness unblunted. Certainly since then rock has become blankly racist, black music increasingly (understandably) cynical. Which is why I don't listen to Otis so much any more – his voice doesn't make sense of today's self-interest and meanness, of the furtive pleasure of good times stalked through Thatcherism. I can't put on his records without this phrase buzzing in my head, sign of changing times and all that, a 1980s epitaph: Otis Redding; Too Good To Be True.

*Otis's classic single 'Dock Of The Bay' sold a million copies within a month of his death.*

# Ronnie Van Zant

## 15 January 1948 - 20 October 1977

## by Chris Charlesworth

*Ronnie Van Zant was born on 15 January 1948 in Jacksonville, Florida. With contemporaries from high school, Van Zant formed Lynyrd Skynyrd in the late sixties. Discovered and signed by Al Kooper, the band supported the Who on their 1973 US tour. They soon gained a reputation as a raunchy rhythm'n'blues-based outfit – an image matched off-stage by their hard drinking and wild behaviour. In their twelve years together, Lynyrd Skynyrd gave 2000 live performances – a record that was only brought to a halt by a fatal plane crash on 20 October 1977. Van Zant and three other members of the group were killed in the accident, on their way to Baton Rouge, Louisiana.*

Ronnie Van Zant was the most powerful singer and charismatic artist to emerge from the school of rock musicians that came out of America's southern states during the early to mid seventies. He was the focal point and principal songwriter in Lynyrd Skynyrd and, indubitably, much more besides: an uncompromising roughneck, a rags to riches hero comparable to Bruce Springsteen and a first class example of that deeply envied accomplishment, the Realization of the American Dream.

For Ronnie to have been killed in

an aeroplane crash just as his musical career was reaching its zenith is as cruel a twist of fortune as any in the history of rock. Over the previous decade he had led Lynyrd Skynyrd with an acute sense of his own particular strength, the crucial ability to progress without compromise, to sail against the current without ever backing down and to fly in the face of prevailing fashion in the certainty that his own vision was both clear and virtuous. 'I have nothing against glitter bands or groups that wear make-up,' he

said in the days when such accoutrements were an indispensable ingredient of rock stardom. 'But that doesn't mean I'll go drinking with them.'

Few bands worked harder (or justified their popularity more) than Lynyrd Skynyrd and Ronnie Van Zant. They spent a dozen years together, sharing good times and bad, and during those years made almost 2,000 live appearances, mostly on American soil. By the summer of 1977 their career was at the crucial stage where creative endeavour and popular acclaim fuse together in the final surge to superstar status. Their 1976 live album *One More From The Road* had sold a million and a half copies and advance orders for their upcoming studio set *Street Survivors* exceeded one million.

In October 1977, the month that this album was released, the group began a lengthy US tour with three shows in their home state of Florida and on October 19 flew north for a concert at the Greenville Memorial Auditorium in South Carolina. The following evening, en route

*A modern day cowboy, Ronnie took off his boots to sing so that he could feel the stage burn.*

for Baton Rouge in Louisiana, their chartered plane crashed near McComb, Mississippi, killing Ronnie, guitarist Steven Gaines and his sister Cassie (one of two back-up vocalists), road manager and close personal friend Dean Kilpatrick and the crew of two. Lynyrd Skynyrd was no more.

It was not the sort of rock death to make newspaper headlines. It had nothing to do with drugs, there was no evidence of foul play and death did not result from over-indulgence in spectacular hedonism. In any case Ronnie's name was not yet known outside the relatively confined world of rock music. For those inside that world, however, Ronnie's death was an appalling shock.

Ronnie epitomized the free-booting style from which Lynyrd Skynyrd drew their inspiration. Rarely seen wearing anything other than a black T-shirt, jeans and broad rimmed hat, he was light on culture but heavy on swagger, a modern day cowboy who took off his boots to sing because, he said, he liked to feel the stage burn when his band was playing. Some say he was flat out on his back, drunk as a skunk on Jack Daniels, when the plane crashed; that he passed away without ever realizing the plane was going down.

All seven members of the original group – Van Zant, Gary Rossington, Allen Collins and Ed King (guitars), Billy Powell (keyboards), Leon Wilkeson (bass) and Bob Burns (drums) – were raised in Jacksonville at the north eastern tip of Florida and they all attended the same high school. They took their name from a master at the school, one Leonard Skinner, who punished them repeatedly for truancy and the length of their hair. Ronnie, the first of three sons born to Lacy Van Zant, was the undisputed leader from the outset. He had been introduced to folk and

blues music from an early age and though he never learned to play an instrument himself he was pleasantly surprised to discover that he had inherited his father's gift for carrying a tune; his innate self-confidence made him a natural choice for front man in the group now formed from these former high school friends.

In the very beginning – during the mid to late sixties – Ronnie's group worked clubs and bars in the Florida area under various names: the Noble Five (before King and Powell joined), the Wild Things and the One Per Cent. Extending their boundaries by 1972, they were spotted in an Atlanta bar by Al Kooper, the former guitarist and keyboard player with the Blues Project and session player for Bob Dylan (among others), who was on the lookout for talent to sign to his newly formed Sounds Of The South record label to be distributed by MCA. Prior to this, Skynyrd had cut a number of sides at the Muscle Shoals Sound Studios but failed to land a record contract.

Kooper produced their debut set *Pronounced Leh-nerd Skin-nerd* and follow-up *Second Helping*. The first contained 'Freebird', a song of soaring beauty which, in concert, became the group's tour de force, a lengthy epic which opened as a mournful blues and closed, ten minutes later, with the frantic three pronged guitar duel which soon became the band's trademark. The second album, arguably their best ever, with the band at its chunky height, contained 'Sweet Home Alabama', a blistering rocker that attacked bigotry, eulogizing the Southern States and proudly declaiming Neil Young's 'Southern Man'. It was a hit single – Skynyrd's only real single success – during 1974. *Second Helping* also contained their anti-drug song 'The Needle And The Spoon' and the tongue-in-cheek boogie 'Work-

ing For MCA'.

By this time Lynyrd Skynyrd had become a popular concert attraction and, in 1973, toured the US supporting the Who on the latter's disappointing *Quadrophenia* tour. Shortly afterwards they disassociated themselves from Kooper and were managed by Peter Rudge, the Who's Cambridge educated US manager and, at that time, a powerful figure in the rock industry. Realizing that their greatest chance of success lay in working live, Rudge arranged a back-breaking series of concert tours between 1974 and 1976, up to 300 shows a year in the US, Japan and Europe. Two British tours and an appearance at the Rolling Stones' massive outdoor Knebworth concert in 1976 ensured them an enthusiastic following in the UK.

They had by this time usurped the popularity once enjoyed by the Allman Brothers Band as the premier rock band from those American States below the Mason-Dixon line. The demise of the Allmans, accelerated by the tragic deaths of Duane Allman and Berry Oakley, was reflected in the deterioration of their music into a lazy parody of former days, and Skynyrd simultaneously drove forward into the clear field ahead. The advent of big money was a further factor in the Allmans' decline; hunger had always fired Van Zant to succeed – and to succeed on his own terms.

The aggression of their live performance was matched by their reputation as hard drinking, fist throwing good ol' southern boys off stage. Stories of their violent behaviour – to each other as well as to outsiders – became a regular feature of their press coverage, while a year never seemed to pass without at least one member of the group totalling a car (and appearing on stage in a plaster cast as a result) or winding up in jail on a drunk and disorderly charge.

Conversely, Ronnie Van Zant's favourite pastime was fishing on the north Florida lakes and everglades. He wrote the lyrics to Skynyrd's songs on these expeditions and enjoyed the contrast between an angler's tranquillity and a rock 'n'roller's tempestuous life-style. When he married he became a conscientious family man, a firm believer in the traditional southern maxim that the man of the household must provide for his kin.

Tom Dowd produced the group's third and fourth albums *Nuthin' Fancy* (1975) and *Gimme Back My Bullets* (1976) but neither rocked as fiercely as the first two sets. The bulk of the material on their live double album *One More From The Road* was drawn from the first two LPs – an indication that creative growth had been temporarily stymied by the incessant touring and consequent popular appeal. Little time had been set aside for writing and, when a free month was available, fatigue eroded their inspiration.

*Street Survivors*, their final album, was preceded by a lengthy (for them) lay-off from road work and the result was a minor triumph, their best album since *Second Helping*, albeit an augury for the future. 'That Smell' was a sombre warning about the perils of life in rock'n'roll and 'You Got That Right' stubbornly defended their aggressive attitude to life in general. Incoming guitarist Steve Gaines had a lion's share in the writing credits and seemed likely to continue as an important figure in the group's creative process.

Within a week of the album's release Lynyrd Skynyrd were no more. Nineteen days after the plane crash the group would have headlined at New York's Madison Square Garden for the first time in their career. Instead prayers were being said for Ronnie Van Zant at a moving funeral service in Jackson-

*Ronnie Van Zant was the focal point and principal songwriter in Lynyrd Skynyrd.*

ville and a prolonged inquest into the cause of the crash was just beginning. Because there was no fire it was assumed that the plane ran out of fuel and in the coming months a sackful of lawsuits were exchanged. Twenty-six people were aboard the flight and, aside from the fatalities, by far the worst injuries were sustained by the other members of the group, who were sitting at the front of the plane.

The tragedy was beset with ironies. The sleeve photograph on the cover of *Street Survivors* depicted the group in a sheet of flame and included within the package was a marketing pamphlet headed 'The Lynyrd Skynyrd Survival Kit'. Rumours that the plane was unfit to fly persisted for some weeks and it was even suggested that Ronnie Van Zant had already spoken of his unwillingness to travel on the plane for the entire tour. Since both pilots were killed the question of the plane's airworthiness was never fully resolved.

One year later an album called *First And....Last* was released and it contained some of Ronnie's best ever writing. It was recorded in Muscle Shoals before Al Kooper discovered Lynyrd Skynyrd and its best song, 'Was I Right', is Van Zant's truest epitaph: the singer, rejected by his family, returns home after finding success to discover his parents dead.

A re-released picture single of 'Freebird' in all its live glory charted in the UK during 1982 and the song has rightly become an FM standard in the US and a perennial favourite among hard rock fans the world over. 'If I leave here tomorrow, Will you still remember me,' Ronnie sings over a fractured keyboard phrase and strained blues guitar. The emotional content and curiously macabre lyric, appropriate though it may be, is a fitting tribute to a singer whose moment of glory was snatched from his grasp at the last moment but whose memory continues to inspire musicians to whom the soft option is anathema to the spirit of rock'n'roll.

# Sid Vicious

## 10 May 1958 - 2 February 1979

## by Nick Kent

*Sid Vicious was born John Simon Ritchie on 10 May 1958 in the East End of London. At Technical College he met John Lydon (Johnny Rotten) who recruited him into the Sex Pistols in March 1977 and renamed him Sid Vicious. With no musical training and only a violent punk image to offer, Vicious had few prospects when the controversial era of the Pistols came to a sudden end. With groupie girlfriend Nancy Spungen he turned to heroin. The violence of his behaviour did not subside when he moved to New York with Spungen, and culminated in his arrest for her murder on 12 October 1978. Released on bail, Vicious was rearrested in December after a night club fight and placed in Rykers Island prison. He was released on bail again on 2 February 1979, but within 24 hours, he was dead from a heroin overdose.*

January 1978, Sticksville, USA, through whose dark heart a bus travels bearing the fabulous Sex Pistols on a tour that will conclude with the group's self-detonation. A deluxe vehicle, its inhabitants comprise the four Pistols, one Malcolm McLaren, some roadies, a Warner Brothers exec and two photographers. Anyway, Sid Vicious is staring out the window – the obligatory beer can in one paw, a sandwich in the other, a blow job on his mind and dreams of a syringe in his arm – when he turns and those scrawny eyes alight on a wondrous vision. Motorcycle boots, to be precise, but not just any old motorcyle boots – these, like, unbelievably heavy-duty storm-trooping creations of leather and steel. They were, however, being worn by one of the photographers; some blinkin' yank called Bob that McLaren was matey with or something. Sid didn't dislike this bloke, mind, didn't much like him, probably.

He meant fuck all to Sid really, he was just, like, there. But the boots were espied and Sid was smitten. He got well intimate then. Nothing extravagant of course, just yer basic, 'Alright then mate? Uh, bet you got some fucking good snaps eh?' Then, with nary a pause, Vicious asked the fellow to flog him his boots, 'cos like, he really fancied 'em'.

Unfortunately, there was a problem here which Sid would have recognized as 'insurmountable' were he, Sid Vicious, capable of comprehending the concept, never mind understanding the word. Bob wasn't some biker fop: it was just that, so spacious were the boots that a whole camera, simply dismantled, would fit snugly inside the lining. They had become a necessary appendage to his vocation. Sid took this in. It's debatable whether he fully grasped the reasons, but he understood a guy saying 'no'. Bob stemmed the tide of pleading he sensed fast approaching by allowing Sid to wear his boots onstage that night at whatever redneck club the group were scheduled to trash.

*In the persona of Sid Vicious, John Simon Ritchie created his own image of one part tortured genius and one part lunatic.*

Once Sid got his feet in Bob's boots he felt himself undergoing a considerable transformation. On the stage that night Sid felt his whole stance increased. The fact that he was performing the wrong bass parts for most of the set was inconsequential. Lydon was acting like a stuck-up wanker, a bloody ponced-up pop star who wasn't, like, even involved in the spirit of the thing. In those boots, those precious boots, Sid felt himself to be invincible. Still, they weren't his.

Bob again allowed Vicious to wear them the next night that the Pistols performed, and *again*, the fact was made resolutely manifest: Sid and these boots were made for each other. He struggled to find the right solution. Bob wasn't budging – this was clear. The boots were back on Bob's feet so stealing them was not feasible. The answer struck home: in order to get those boots, Sid would have to kill him.

It was approaching 3 am and virtually every passenger on this downbound bus was sprawled in positions appropriate to some condition of sleep. Providential indeed, then, that one of the party should awake just in time to look upon a chilling spectacle. Bob was sound asleep in a vaguely upright position, his backbone curved against the slight dip in the posture sprung seating. Directly behind his prone form stood Sid Vicious, his right hand brandishing a Bowie knife.

Amassing what strength he could muster, our interloper managed to tackle Vicious from behind, jerking both arms up behind his (Vicious') head and removing the weapon almost at once. Vicious didn't scream or attempt to unfasten his gangling limbs from the hammer-lock. Amazingly, the action itself roused not a soul, not even Bob. The interloper, a longstanding colleague of McLaren, had encountered Sid on various occasions, though never remotely in such circumstances. He

'You can't arrest me. I'm a rock'n'roll star.'

was stunned. Vicious was also stunned: the interloper's shocked stare bore down on him. The first person to break the silence was Sid. Shamefaced, he pleaded with an earnestness that undermined any possibility of it being a humorous remark. 'I would have woken him before I slit his throat,' he kept repeating.

That is my favourite Sid Vicious story, not simply because it packs that good hearty thwack of sensa-

tionalism, but more because it is a perfect example of the psychological bomb-site upon which John Simon Ritchie invented his own Action Man in the persona of Sid Vicious.

Ritchie was born on 10 May 1958, a suitably turbulent year, that witnessed the lascivious rise and fall of Jerry Lee Lewis, infamy's most indomitable living practitioner, the slayings of young Nebraskan Charlie Starkweather, and the celluloid vision of Elvis Presley, a young god, explaining his physical predilections to some cornfed belle thus:

'That ain't tactics, baby, that's the beast in me.'

He grew up in and around the outskirts of London – principally the East End – the only child of a single parent and, in those crucial seven years of life, well, one can surmise. Imagine claustrophobic estate blocks, spurious influences, and the presence of something inexplicably disturbing, impersonal and sickly-scented; the sight of some stranger laying comatose against a bean-bag. Children around junkies are given few options in life. Our little prince was given two: he could stare at the wall, or he could throw himself against it. He chose the latter, time and time again.

Most rock stars of the rebellious mould use their parents' values as the source point of their desire for reinvention. John Simon Ritchie used the world as a whole, but, lacking vision and the potential to apply himself, his *alter ego* was fashioned more by a colleague, John Lydon. He, Lydon and others were a gang – sneering and puerile with Lydon the brains and the rest the brawn and banter. Because virtually all this mob were called John, making it hard to know whose round it was, nicknames were compulsory. Lydon re-christened our lad Sid – a name he loathed, but duly lived with.

Sid initially adored Lydon, with his higher intellect and a clear cutting edge to his loathing. When the latter was asked to join the Sex Pistols, Sid and the others became a leering gestapo for Lydon's Top Cat persona. Fuelled on leapers (favoured by 90 per cent of bank robbers) they were the big noise now, *they knew the truth* and anyone threatening that autonomy was needful of a lesson in intimidation.

In June of 1976, Sid was dispatched to give such a lesson to a journalist at a Pistols gig taking place in the 100 Club. Assisted by a psychopath accomplice, who held

*Sneering and puerile, Sid could only survive as one of a gang.*

a knife some two inches, no more, from this music writer's face, Sid landed five good scalp-lacerating hits with his rusty bike chain. Only once did he hit his mark, causing much bloodletting, but little damage. The blow, however, warranted an ebullient Lydon to grant Sid a new surname: 'Vicious'.

Infamy was now calling the shots:

Sid was quoted at length in punk exposés; he abhorred 'sex', 'uniforms', 'hypocritical bastards', 'hippies', 'poseurs', prescribing 'a good kicking for all and sundry'. But he only managed to foul up everything he got involved in. No stamina, no gumption. As one quarter of the Sex Pistols – at their best the musical equivalent of a car wreck – he displayed all the dexterity of a one-legged man at an arse-kicking contest. As a hellion, he

*Sid and girlfriend Nancy Spungen outside Marylebone Magistrates Court, where they had appeared on a drugs charge.*

was feeble. Where the desperado or snake-eyed boy lets his weapon do the talking, Vicious would solemnly intone, 'Well, I think that I'm not, like, *really, really* vicious, y'know...' He'd pause, lost in half-baked exegesis, 'but I'm pretty wild'!

Sid Vicious was a dirty fighter. He couldn't throw a punch and lacked the bearing, the stance of a good scrapper. A good scrapper works from his heels, uses his wits, develops a technique for felling his

*Sid Vicious the archetypal punk – angry, inarticulate and given to self-mutilation.*

opponent. Vicious just bottled in, all gangly limbs and mock sneer. He was dangerous because pain – physical pain – wasn't a concern he seemed remotely aware of. Instead he would wantonly gouge his torso with broken glass, razor blades, knife cuts. He would do this when he was 'bored'. Boredom was intolerable, as the great George Sanders pointed out in his suicide note.

Love, for Sid, was another wretched contrivance, be it 'universal harmony' or the more intimate variant. By the autumn of 1976, as an oft-quoted celebrity in the vanguard of punk's disaffected youth, he boasted that he was the most sexless creature in the world. Then, some four months on, he

encountered Nancy Spungen and duly revised his opinion.

Vicious first tried heroin not in the company of Spungen but in the company of Heartbreakers' Johnny Thunders and Jerry Nolan. The former would wave a syringe in the face of some uninitiated, impressionable shill. 'Are you a boy or a man?' he would tease, turning the issue into a matter of machismo. Vicious, of course, tried it – twice, in fact, whilst in their company. He threw up a lot and found the experience less than awe-inspiring. However, when Spungen, a maladjusted harridan who'd flown to London in the vain hope of recommencing her fleeting affair with drummer Nolan, found herself in Vicious' company, she sensed the malleable nature of Vicious' hedonistic potential and steered him into the murky precincts of filtered cottons and that same acrid stench he must have recalled offending his senses as a child. For a short while there was a sexual rapport that Vicious had never believed could exist. The archetypal mixed-up little boy and his maladjusted, self-fixated little girl looking for that golden-armed handshake from a white-knuckled world. Some would call it 'love' – but I prefer to concur with Lou Reed in 'Street Hassle': 'It's called bad luck.'

Infamy is a flint-hearted vocation to live with, requiring lightning reflexes and an abundance of quick wittedness. Vicious and Spungen had neither. Two months of enchantment curdled overnight into a year of entrapment. Romeo and Juliet they weren't: their relationship was closer to the hopelessly juvenile version of Jack Lemmon and Lee Remmick in *Days of Wine and Roses*. On 12 October 1978, ten months after the Pistols' detonation, during which time Vicious had alienated everyone he'd ever known but his soul-mate, the affair came to a predictably gore-spattered conclusion. At 10.50 am, a barely coherent English accent phoned the Chelsea Hotel switchboard asking someone to check room 100 because 'someone is seriously injured'. The Manhattan police arrived to find Vicious stunned, seated on the bed while in the bathroom the dead body of Nancy Spungen lay under the sink, a trail of blood running from the bed to her final resting place. When probed, Vicious stated that the fatality had occurred because he was 'a dog, a dirty dog'. A moment later, suddenly acquainted with the enormity of his circumstances, he said, 'You can't arrest me. I'm a rock'n'roll star.'

Ten days later Sid was free on bail. Old acquaintances had sprung to his aid. His mother had flown over; Malcolm McLaren (who, weeks earlier, had refused to take a phone call from his former client) was in town, determined to free 'his boy' even if it meant employing the services of F. Lee Bailey, America's most prestigious defence lawyer. Conspiracy theories were being tossed around: Spungen had been the victim of a drugs syndicate hit; a mugger had attacked her while Vicious slept. Optimism reigned, or so it seemed, but Vicious was far from jubilant. His metabolism had been through hell while he was ensconced at Ryker's Island jail. Also, his conscience was riddled with a gnawing remorse.

That evening, he locked the door to the bathroom and, finding only a Bic razor and broken lightbulb, he slashed away at every vein in his arms and legs. His mother respected her son's wish to die and sat by him as the blood seeped from his body. By the time McLaren and Joe Stevens, Vicious' unofficial minder, arrived they were confronted with a scene of extraordinary hideousness. Vicious was so far gone he could no longer control his bladder and urine spurted

*The Sex Pistols. Left to right: Paul Cook, Sid Vicious, Johnny Rotten and Steve Jones.*

onto the blood-soaked sheets. Mrs Beverly immediately rounded on a dazed McLaren, informing him that this was a suicide pact and not to interfere. Sid meanwhile, still conscious, begged his manager to go out and score some downers so as to stop the pain. McLaren walked to the door not knowing what to do. Stevens meanwhile knelt next to Vicious and, a small cassette recorder in his hand, pressed 'record'. The first words are his. 'So, Sid, on that night, what really happened?'

The tape lasted half an hour; lapses occurred, the voice receded yet the clarity of recollection was consistent.

They'd been waiting to score having received a wad of dollar bills – over 1,000 in cash – for an upcoming gig. However, no narcotics could be found. Their dealer, Robert, gave them Tuinol, a heavy barbiturate which, mixed with alcohol, caused

Vicious' withdrawal symptoms to worsen. At one point he left the room and began knocking on all the doors of the Chelsea Hotel, screaming for drugs.

This alerted a suitably imposing black custodian, who, having verbally warned Vicious – only to be called 'a fuckin' nigger' – began striking the puny twerp; in the process breaking his nose. Vicious crawled back to the room to be confronted by Spungen, equally enraged. She slapped his face, striking the broken nose and causing the brutish pain to intensify. Vicious, standing by the table on which a seven-inch knife was placed, reciprocated. One clean lunge at the stomach of his beloved: it was hopeless, stupid and typical of their relationship. Minutes later they were embracing, reconciled. Unfortunately, Spungen removed the blade and omitted to cover the wound with a bandage of any sort. She lay down on the bed, while Vicious, similarly negligent in matters of basic hygiene, dashed off to keep an appointment at the Methadone clinic. When he returned, his beloved Nancy was deceased. She was not yet 21. Police duly noted that her corpse was already decomposing a mere seven hours after death.

As Vicious finished the halting recitation, McLaren returned, not with a handful of downers but with an ambulance. Two weeks in Bellevue Hospital had Vicious patched up. His morale also changed: guilt and remorse were no longer concerns worthy of a wild and crazy desperado like Sid Vicious. Like all hopelessly self-absorbed rock stars, he detoured away from moral considerations and believed what he and his fans wanted. He wasn't guilty and the realization that he was once more a big noise – possibly capable of literally getting away with murder – excited him. He had a new girlfriend, Michelle Robinson, another groupie, and that cocky psychopathic attitude – *'I'm a rock'n'roll star. You can't arrest me'* – was suddenly back to the forefront.

It ended on the second week of December 1978. Vicious, back to his initial kamikaze oafishness, had lewdly propositioned the girlfriend of Todd Smith, brother of Patti. Smith had verbally reprimanded him only to have Vicious smash a broken bottle into his face, almost blinding him. Smith pressed charges and Vicious was back in Ryker's Island alongside the 'niggers' who beat him bloody, the 'spicks' who spat at him, the hardcore bad arse elite who took no truck from some fucked-up limey pop star whose choices and options they never had. In Ryker's Island, punks weren't spiky-haired rebels with guitars and wild, crazy attitudes. They were the broken spirits, the losers who could only survive via homosexual liaisons which would offer them protection.

*With Johnny Thunders in New York. When the Pistols split up Sid had nothing to offer but the myth of his empty stardom.*

Vicious was released almost two months later, on 2 February. He boasted to Jerry Nolan that he'd gotten on well with his cohabitants; that these desperados could see that he, Vicious, was cut from the same leathery fabric as themselves. In reality, he had been treated like scum. Arriving at a celebratory bash, clean and in good spirits, he injected some heroin his mother had bought for him, fearing he'd try scoring himself, thus jeopardizing his bail again. He immediately blacked out, his complexion tinged with the blue signs of overdose – but, after a short exercise, he came to and continued, in good spirits, to muse about the future.

Yes, he could still fantasize. But then reality would impinge and

he'd realize that no matter which defence lawyer was involved, no matter how much he could kid himself he was innocent, it was over. No, Ryker's Island was not going to see him languishing with other lifers, perverts and losers. While Robinson slept, he found another packet of the deadly powder. This time there was no-one conscious to awaken him from falling into the abyss. He heated the spoon, filtered the cotton and – his life revolving around him – turned to dust. The scum that also rises sank into an unmarked grave.

Decomposing was their greatest achievement. A mere seven hours after expiring, Nancy Spungen was already smelling of death. It takes up to 48 hours before the putrifying odour commences in corpses of the old. At the age of twenty, both had wasted themselves beyond belief. Let them rot.

# Gene Vincent

## 11 February 1935 - 12 October 1971

## by Mick Farren

*Gene Vincent was born on 11 February 1935 in Norfolk, Virginia. He began to sing while recovering from a motorcycle accident, which left him lame for life. Vilified in the US for his hell-raising on and off-stage, Vincent moved to Britain where he enjoyed his most sustained success. His one great hit was 'Be-Bop-A-Lula'. In 1960, he went on a UK tour with Eddie Cochran and was involved in a serious car crash which killed Cochran and worsened Vincent's leg injury. He subsequently suffered the effects of serious drinking and his musical career rapidly deteriorated until he was reduced to playing village fetes in France. He went back to the US in 1971 and a few days later, on 12 October 1971, he died of a seizure resulting from a perforated ulcer.*

I've never been too enthusiastic about the common fantasy of rock'n'roll heaven. It's a cheap cliché, watered-down Milton, Sunday School metaphysics. Worst of all, it's potentially as boring as it's unworkable. Who in their right mind takes any kind of comfort from imagining Buddy Holly dressed in a white suit, sitting on a cloud, strumming the introduction to 'Maybe Baby' over and over again, all the way to infinity? Do you think either Elvis Presley

or Keith Moon would be ambulatory, let alone coherent? Would Jimi Hendrix want to hang out with Jim Morrison after what went down at Steve Paul's Scene that night in 1969? Would you really want all these inadequate, self destructive dopefiend neurotics to spend their afterlife up to their knees in Hammer Film mist playing in some morbid eternal jam session?

About the only sympathetic detail in the whole dreary concept is that perhaps somewhere there's a dark corner where Hank Williams and

Gene Vincent could drink bourbon and pop pills and talk without feeling the need to listen.

Gene Vincent and Hank Williams had more than enough in common to make it a plausible liaison. Hank had a painfully deformed spine. Gene Vincent had a crippled leg. They both had high nasal southern boy voices that had brought them fame and fortune long before they had any clue about how to handle it. They were plagued by wives and managers who took advantage of the all-consuming carelessness with which they handled their affairs. They both looked to speed and whisky for insulation from the rigours of pop and pain. In the end, the combination would kill them both. Gene and Hank would have plenty to talk about.

Hank was indisputedly the greater talent. That's why he ended up as a hallowed icon of country music. That's why they keep his boots in the Country Music Hall of Fame in Nashville. Gene Vincent wasn't so much a talent as a source of divine energy. That's why he would have to be content with

*Vincent's pasty complexion, his black leather clothes and greased-back hair guaranteed that he would never go unnoticed.*

recognition as one of the romantic bad boys of rock'n'roll. That's why Gene Vincent's boots are the prized possession of a middle-aged biker in San Bernardino.

The first time I saw Gene Vincent, I was but a youth. It must have been one of my very first rock concerts. The tour had started as a double-header, Gene Vincent and Eddie Cochran. By the time it reached the Brighton Essoldo, Eddie Cochran was something like a month dead and his place on the bill had been taken by an individual called Jerry Keller who was having his fifteen minutes of fame with a tune called 'Here Comes Summer' (school is out, oh happy day...). Needless to say, he received short shrift from the Teds and greasers, the Triumph Bonneville school of criticism, who made up what seemed like 90 per cent of the audience. All memory of him has been completely blotted out. Gene, on the other hand, has remained indelibly engraved. He was the performer, who finally removed any doubts I might have had that rock'n'roll was, when you got down to basics, about anything else but the nasty side of life.

Vincent came on in the first top-to-toe black leather suit that I'd ever seen. There was a ring on the outside of his single black glove. His collar was turned up in the back and framed an immaculate DA. An equally perfect bunch of grapes cascaded down his forehead. A gold chain with a heavy gold medallion hung around his neck. He moved with an accentuated limp. The end of a steel leg brace was clearly visible below the cuff of his pants. He looked like Richard III updated for the era of the Sabre jet. (TV producer Jack Good has since taken nearly total credit for the look but, in my experience, Gene Vincent may have been crazy but he wasn't anyone's puppet.) If, in the teen myths of the time, Elvis Presley was the leader of the pack, Gene Vincent

*Gene Vincent with ex-Shadow Jet Harris.*

was the psychotic cripple kid who you could bet on being shot dead by the cops well before the end of the last reel.

On stage, he was backed by Sounds Incorporated who, at the time, were rated as the most professional of the big tour back-up bands. They had a reputation for consistent quality that would soon take them to the USA to open for the Beatles. Their fat horn section gave them a depth and solidity that were lacking in the contemporary guitar bands typified by Cliff Richard's Shadows and Billy Fury's Tornadoes. Vincent took all that they could give him and projected it out to the crowd with an intensity that threatened to burn him up. His face was contorted and corpse white. His eyes would swivel heavenwards and he'd appear to quiver as though racked by the energy that was passing through

him. With one leg in a brace, Gene couldn't shake like Elvis. From the waist down he was rigid, his damaged leg stuck out behind him. He clung to the microphone for dear life. At moments of extreme stage passion, he would spin through 360 degrees and swing his crippled leg clean over the mike. Like I said before, he radiated nasty. He sang of nasty love with girls in tight skirts and red lipstick, his attitude was one of frantically mindless, nasty juvenile aggression. He had no time for the teenage euphemisms used by the 'acceptable' rock stars. Gene didn't give a damn about being acceptable. He had enough problems just singing out his demons.

When I saw the leather-clad Vincent all those years ago I was in fact witnessing what amounted to the peak of his second career. In America, he had already soared and fallen, a victim of the back-lash against hard rock which had also pushed Jerry Lee Lewis and Little Richard out of the limelight. The Gene Vincent story is not particularly complicated. He was born Eugene Vincent Craddock on 11 February 1935 in the rough tough Navy port of Norfolk, Virginia. At 17, he took the line of least resistance and joined the Navy. Although singing was a hobby, the Navy offered the minimal security of three square meals a day and not having to think for yourself. Away from the stage, Gene Vincent was neither very swift nor very smart. His naval career was undistinguished. He served on a tanker, the USS *Chuckwan*, a tender, the USS *Tutuwla*, and a landing craft that didn't even merit a name, the LST 581.

Vincent might have remained a lifetime sailor except for a motorcycle accident while he was on shore leave in Norfolk in 1955. A young woman in a Chrysler ran through a red light and broadsided Gene and his Harley Davidson. The left hand side of his bike was completely mashed and Vincent's leg was all but severed at the shin. The injury meant the end of his career in the service. All he had to look forward to was a lengthy series of operations and a long convalescence. The accident was also the act of fate that would turn him into a rock star. Fate, however, doesn't always deal a uniformly benign hand. The pain and complications caused by Vincent's subsequent neglect of his leg would be the root cause of the drinking and drug abuse that would eventually kill him.

At this point, though, the pain and unpleasantness were a long way in the future. The 21-year-old Vincent used the long stay in naval hospitals and the Navy disability cheques to concentrate seriously on his singing. While still on crutches, he was working a regular Saturday night spot on WCMS radio.

At WCMS, he attracted the attention of a dubious character, a disc jockey on the station called 'Sheriff' Tex Davis, who saw himself as the Colonel Tom Parker figure in Gene Vincent's life.

Although later Davis would be accused of the most hideous mismanagement and the virtual wrecking of Gene's career, he was responsible for the initial coup that won Vincent and his band, the Bluecaps, a contract with Capitol Records. Demos made at WCMS were brought to the notice of Ken Nelson at Capitol, an executive who had just lost out in the bidding for Elvis Presley's contract. He was one of the few people at Capitol who perceived that the label was suffering from a rock'n'roll gap and that the corporate policy of totally hitching their fortunes to traditional acts like Dean Martin and Kay Starr was a courtship with disaster. Nelson jumped at the chance to sign a bona fide, carpet-chewing rock'n'roller.

Despite Nelson's enthusiasm, Capitol was hardly the right environment for Vincent. Although he cut seven albums for the label, he was always treated with an air of disdain. If it hadn't been for the fact that Gene made money, they wouldn't have let him anywhere near them. In Capitol's eyes, he was an ignorant, anti-social punk with a drinking problem, the very last kind of being that they wanted dirtying up their nice clean Hollywood tower. Eight months after signing Vincent, Capitol discovered a rock star with whom they could empathize. Tommy Sands was a Pat Boone clone who had a brief marriage to Nancy Sinatra and then vanished into that great limbo that awaits the once nearly famous.

The phenomenal success of his single, 'Be-Bop-A-Lula', catapulted Gene to international recognition; unfortunately, a combination of Tex's mismanagement and his and the Bluecaps transcendental disre-

gard for contemporary standards of decency dumped him right back into the sweating drudgery of non-stop minor league touring. To be fair, there weren't too many places that someone like Gene Vincent could go. For better or worse, Elvis had set off for Hollywood and chicken respectability, Pat Boone had gone to church. These were not alternatives for Gene. He had a band who caused pregnancies and set fire to motels. He had even threatened to punch up the all-powerful Dick Clark and got himself blacklisted from 'American Bandstand'. The only people who liked Gene Vincent were the kids themselves. To the mass entertainment industry, he was poison, beyond all hope of redemption.

Juvey Gomez was one of the long line of drummers with the Blue Caps. In an interview, he describes a not atypical Saturday night on the road: 'The motel manager had found out that we'd destroyed one of his rooms so the sheriff and his deputy came over and they pulled Gene off – off the stage! They booked him for wrecking a motel room, being drunk around minors and doing a lewd show. They dragged him off stage physically – bodily – and took him to jail and nobody had enough money to bail him out, so we had to wire to Dallas for some money and they got it there barely in time to get him out to the National Guard Armoury gig we had that same night. So we got to the Armoury and the place was jammed full of drunken Indians and Mexicans and half breeds, a few little white people scattered around and two black couples. And one of the black guys asked somebody else to dance, somebody else didn't like it and so they started a fight. The whole thing erupted and so the sheriff came back out and shot tear gas bombs in the place and cleared it – packed it with tear gas.'

By the end of the fifties Vincent

no longer had a viable career in the USA. He wasn't alone – Jerry Lee Lewis, Eddie Cochran and a whole bunch of lesser performers had been eased out of mass market pop in favour of the Bobbies and the Frankies and the Fabians who were all pledged to remain high school, wholesome teenagers.

Gene's move to Europe was one of the few sensible decisions he ever made. There he was still considered a wild man, but he was an exotic wild man from across the water, a genuine rock'n'roll cowboy and infinitely superior to the contemporary homegrown product. In Britain, France and Germany, he became the king of the embryonic but rapidly growing concert circuit. The up-and-coming of the time, led by John Lennon and Paul McCartney, beat a path to his dressing room door to hug Gene and have their pictures taken for *Merseybeat*.

Europe may have given Gene a new lease of life, but it didn't stop the abuses of the past catching up with him. At no point since the motorcycle accident in Norfolk had Gene stayed anywhere long enough to allow the injuries to his leg to heal properly. The recurrent complications became chronic. From time to time, he'd attend a hospital in a fleeting attempt to have his leg fixed once and for all, but his lack of patience and the demands of his career never allowed him the time to let the healing process complete itself. His primary defence against the almost constant pain was increasing amounts of booze and pills. His life once again began to deteriorate. He broke his collarbone in the car crash that killed his friend Eddie Cochran. His marriage failed and, for a while, the British authorities denied him a work permit. Associates recount how he spent a lot of time in an incoherent daze. In London and Paris, he was a regular sight in the sleazier GI after-hours

*Above and opposite: On stage Vincent was intense, passionate, threatening.*

joints.

By the mid-sixties, in the face of first the mods and then the hippies, Gene Vincent became something of an anachronism. His drinking had caused him to put on a lot of weight and as he slowed down, his act included more and more dragged-out, low tempo country music. Dark, paranoid fantasies began to close in on him. He held up an elevator full of people with a shotgun in a London hotel where his wife was hiding from him. He seemed to be convinced that, right from the start, there had been a sinister conspiracy to destroy his career. When I talked to him in 1969, he was convinced that Eddie Cochran had survived the auto crash only to be murdered in the ambulance by a British promoter who had a piece of his future royalties.

The rock revival at the end of the sixties provided Gene with one final shot. Jim Morrison – who certainly owed Vincent a debt of gratitude for the loan of both his pose and his wardrobe – Kim Fowley and DJ John

Peel rallied around to bring Vincent virtually back from the dead. He cut an album for Elektra and appeared at the 1969 Toronto Rock Festival, but long term salvage proved impossible. In 1971, he died after a seizure caused by bleeding ulcers. The booze had finally got him.

Gene Vincent wasn't one of rock'n'roll's greatest talents. His voice was limited and his attempts at songwriting were rudimentary. He is, however, one of its major legends. He tapped the very essence of rock'n'roll. In his prime, he was a violent, hellraising kid who had only anger and excitement to talk about. He wasn't sufficiently articulate to explain his rebellion, he simply hit out at whatever moved and if he missed he took a drink and tried again. If he contributed anything to rock'n'roll it was an attitude, the surly confidence that, in rock music, here finally was a land where there didn't need to be rules. It was a new game in which anyone could play. Fuck them if they couldn't take a joke. It was fitting that, with Ian Dury's 'Sweet Gene Vincent', the most appropriate tribute to him was paid by rock'n'roll itself.

# The Artists

DUANE ALLMAN, along with brother Gregg, formed the Allman Brothers Band in the late sixties, and was hailed as one of the world's leading exponents of bottleneck guitar. He died in a motorcycle accident in 1971 aged 24.

MARC BOLAN first enjoyed mainstream success as frontman of the glam rock band T. Rex. Poised to make a comeback in 1977 after the group's popularity had slumped, he was killed in a car crash aged 29.

TOMMY BOLIN played guitar with several small bands before joining Deep Purple in 1975, when he replaced Ritchie Blackmore. He died of drug abuse in 1976 aged 25.

JOHN BONHAM joined the New Yardbirds in 1968. Under their new name, Led Zeppelin, Bonham earned his reputation as the heavy metal drummer. He died from asphyxiation after a heavy drinking session in 1980 aged 32.

EDDIE COCHRAN was one of the original rockers. Inspired by Elvis, he turned from hillbilly to rock'n'roll and had his first hit single in 1958. He was killed in a car crash in 1960 aged 21.

SAM COOKE originally sang gospel before turning to rhythm'n'blues in 1957. A gifted singer and songsmith, he had a string of hit singles before being shot dead in 1964 aged 33.

IAN CURTIS was singer and lyricist with punk band Warsaw, who changed their name to Joy Division in 1978, and became a leading light in the New Wave era. He committed suicide in 1980 aged 23.

SANDY DENNY sang with the Strawbs and Fairport Convention before forming her own band Fotheringay in 1970. She rejoined Fairport Convention in 1974 and left to go solo two years later. She died after a fall in 1978 aged 31.

MAMA CASS ELLIOT sang on the folk circuit before joining the Mamas and the Papas in 1965. The group split up in 1968 when Cass left to pursue a solo career. She died in 1974 of a heart attack aged 32.

MARVIN GAYE was one of Tamla Motown's leading male vocalists from the early sixties to his departure from the label in 1983. He was shot dead by his father on the eve of his 45th birthday.

LOWELL GEORGE played guitar with Factory and Frank Zappa before forming cult band Little Feat in 1970. The group split up in 1975 when George turned solo. He died in 1979 of a heart attack aged 34.

JIMI HENDRIX has been one of the most influential and imitated electric guitarists of all time. The Monterey and Woodstock pop festivals made him a legend, but he died from a drug overdose in 1970 aged 27.

BUDDY HOLLY formed his band the Crickets in 1957, scoring several hits with them before embarking on a solo tour in 1959. He died in a plane crash en route to one of his concerts aged 22.

BRIAN JONES helped found the Rolling Stones in 1963. In June 1969 he announced his departure from the band and a month later drowned in his swimming pool aged 27.

JANIS JOPLIN became a star after the Monterey pop festival in 1967 and began her solo singing career the following year. In spite of her success she was depressed and died from a drug overdose in 1970 aged 27.

JOHN LENNON founded his first group in 1960, out of which grew the Beatles. The band stayed together until 1970, when Lennon turned solo. He was shot dead in 1980 aged 40.

BOB MARLEY formed reggae group the Wailers in 1963, and became the first reggae superstar, bringing the music to a much wider audience. He died of a brain tumour in 1981 aged 36.

RON 'PIGPEN' McKERNAN was the singer and keyboard player with the Grateful Dead. By 1971 heavy drinking had forced him to leave the group, and he died in 1973 from a stomach haemorrhage aged 27.

KEITH MOON joined the Who as their drummer in 1964. Known as the wild man of rock, he died from an overdose of sedatives in 1975 aged 31.

JIM MORRISON formed the Doors in 1965 and took the role of singer and lyricist. He left the band and retired to Paris in 1971 where he died of a heart attack aged 27.

GRAM PARSONS began singing protest songs in his teens. He helped create country rock and spent time playing with the Byrds and Emmylou Harris. He died from an overdose in 1973 aged 26.

ELVIS PRESLEY signed his first record contract in 1955 and scored hit after hit for the next 20 years. He died in 1977 of a heart attack aged 42.

OTIS REDDING won a contract with Stax records in 1962, and by 1965 was their top solo soul singer. The Monterey pop festival in 1967 made him a star with rock audiences, but he died later that year in a plane crash aged 26.

RONNIE VAN ZANT formed Lynyrd Skynyrd in the late sixties. They gained a reputation for raunchy rhythm'n'blues but in 1977 Van Zant, aged 29, and other members of the band were killed in a plane crash.

*SID VICIOUS joined the Sex Pistols in 1977 and, on their break-up in 1978, moved to New York. While on bail, accused of murdering his girlfriend, he died from a heroin overdose in 1979 aged 20.*

*GENE VINCENT began singing rock 'n'roll in the late fifties. Renowned for his hell-raising on and off-stage, he died of a seizure in 1971 aged 36.*

# The Contributors

*CHRIS CHARLESWORTH was a staff writer for* Melody Maker *for six years before taking up an appointment with the management company which handled Lynyrd Skynyrd. He has also written several books relating to music and now works as an editor in publishing.*

*JOHN COLLIS was rock music editor for* Time Out *magazine, and has published Buddy Holly and Eddie Cochran song books, as well as being editor and contributor to* The Rock Primer.

*CAMERON CROWE is an associate editor of* Rolling Stone *and is an expert on southern rock music and musicians. He is also the author of* Stairway To Heaven: A Year In High School.

*DAVID DALTON was an associate editor at* Rolling Stone *and is the author of* James Dean: The Mutant King, The Rolling Stones: The First Twenty Years *and* Janis Joplin: Piece Of My Heart. *He is also co-author of* James Dean: American Icon *and* Rock 100. *He is now writing plays and screenplays.*

*BRIAN EDGE is the author of* New Order And Joy Division: Pleasures And Wayward Distractions *and has written a book on the Fall entitled* Paintwork.

*MICK FARREN is the co-author of* Elvis: The Complete Illustrated Record *and author of* The Black Leather Jacket. *He has also compiled* Elvis In His Own Words. *He is a well-known science fiction novelist and has been writing about popular culture since the late sixties.*

*BEN FONG-TORRES was an editor of* Rolling Stone *from 1969 to 1980 and has written extensively on the Californian rock scene. He is the co-editor of* The Rolling Stone Interviews *and editor of* What's That Sound? Readings In Contemporary Music.

*DAVID FRICKE is the American correspondent for* Melody Maker. *He is a regular contributor on heavy metal for* Rolling Stone *and* Trouser Press.

*SIMON FRITH has written about music for many years in numerous publications. He has been a columnist for* Creem *and* Melody Maker *and was rock music editor at the* Sunday Times. *He currently writes for the* Village Voice *and for the* Observer *and is the author of two books –* Sound Effects *and* Music For Pleasure.

*PAULO HEWITT is a staff writer for* New Musical Express.

*JERRY HOPKINS is the co-author of the Jim Morrison biography* No One Here Gets Out Alive *with Danny Sugerman. He has written two books on Elvis Presley –* Elvis *and* Elvis: The Final Years *and is also author of* Bowie, Yoko Ono *and* The Jimi Hendrix Story. *He was a contributing editor at* Rolling Stone *for fifteen years.*

*PATRICK HUMPHRIES is the author of five books, among them* Meet On The Ledge: A History Of Fairport Convention *and* Bruce Springsteen: Blinded By The Light. *He is now a freelance music journalist and has written for such publications as* Rolling Stone, Melody Maker, *the* Listener, Blitz *and the* London Evening Standard.

*NICK KENT was a regular contributor to* New Musical Express *between 1972 and 1981. He is now a freelance writer and contributes to* Creem, Rolling Stone *and the* Face.

*GREIL MARCUS was an associate editor at* Rolling Stone *and has written for many other publications, among them the* Village Voice, *and the* New Yorker. *He is author of* Mystery Train: Images of America

In Rock'n'Roll Music *and* Lipstick Traces. *He is editor of* Stranded.

*GAVIN MARTIN is a staff writer for* New Musical Express.

*PHILIP NORMAN is the author of the best-selling biography of the Rolling Stones,* The Stones *and the history of the Beatles,* Shout! *and has conducted exclusive interviews with Yoko Ono.*

*MARK PAYTRESS is the features editor at* Record Collector Magazine. *His book* Entranced: The Siouxsie And The Banshees Story *will be published later this year.*

*BUD SCOPPA has contributed to* Rolling Stone *among many other publications. He is the author of* The Byrds *and* Rock People. *He is currently a writer in the press department of A & M records.*

*CHARLES SHAAR MURRAY is the co-author with Roy Carr of* David Bowie: An Illustrated Record. *He was an editor at* New Musical Express *and is now a freelance writer, contributing to the* Observer Section 5 *and* Q Magazine.

*JOHN SWENSON has written for a number of publications, among them* Rolling Stone, Crawdaddy, Creem *and* Sounds. *He is the co-author of* The Rolling Stone Record Guide *and author of* The Rolling Stone Guide To Jazz Records *and* Stevie Wonder.

*JOHN TOBLER is the author of* The Buddy Holly Story, *and has contributed to numerous magazines and music publications. He is also the author of* Guitar Greats *and* The Record Producers, *which he wrote after the highly successful BBC radio series.*

*CLIFF WHITE was a freelance writer for many years before he joined Charly Records to become their press and promotions officer, compiling outstanding rec-* ord collections from the Charly archives. *He now works for Demon Records.*

*TIM WHITE was formerly a contributing editor for* Rolling Stone *and managing editor of* Crawdaddy. *He is the author of* Catch A Fire: The Life of Bob Marley *and* Rock Stars *and now writes for* Atlantic Monthly.